Keeping Kids Safe

A GUIDE FOR PARENTS OF TODDLERS AND TEENS — AND ALL THE YEARS IN BETWEEN

Dr. Kenneth Shore

Family and Educational Psychologist

Prentice Hall Press

Library of Congress Cataloging-in-Publication Data

Shore, Kenneth.
 Keeping kids safe : a guide for parents of toddlers and teens,
 and all the years in between / Kenneth Shore.
   p. cm.
 Includes bibliographical references and index.
 ISBN 0-7352-0214-1 (paper)
   1. Children's accidents—Prevention.   I. Title.

HV675.72.S48 2001
649'.4—dc21

2001035298

Acquisitions Editor: *Gloria Fuzia*
Production Editor: *Sharon Gonzalez*
Interior Design/Page Layout: *Dimitra Coroneos*

Printed in the United States of America

10 9 8 7 6 5 4 3 2 1

ISBN 0-7352-0214-1

 Prentice Hall Press Paramus, NJ 07652

http://www.phdirect.com

Contents

In memory of my father
Michael Shore

Introduction

Parenting a child in today's world poses a considerable challenge. Foremost among the concerns of most parents is their children's safety. Only when parents have peace of mind that their children are safe and secure can they begin to enjoy raising them. Only when they are confident that their children are not in harm's way can they relax and begin to focus on parenting's pleasures rather than its perils.

As the following results of various studies and surveys show, many of the safety concerns of parents are well founded.

In school or child care settings:

- Child care at most centers is of poor to mediocre quality, according to experts in the field.

- More than one in three students say they do not feel safe at school.

- Fifteen to twenty percent of all students are victimized by bullies at some point in their school careers.

Outside of school:

- Approximately one of every seven children between the ages of five and twelve spends time unsupervised after school.

- About fifty percent of sixth graders say they feel pressure from peers to drink alcohol.

- There are nearly thirty thousand active gangs in this country, targeting children as young as ten for membership.

In their communities:

- Each day on average twelve children ages one to nineteen are killed by gunfire.

- Approximately one in five girls and one in seven boys are sexually abused before turning eighteen.

In the world of electronic media:

- Children's television programs contain more violence than any other form of television programming.

- About one in four children has received unwanted exposure to sexually explicit pictures while surfing the Internet.

Parents must assume primary responsibility for protecting their children. The challenge you, as a parent, face is to provide your children with the knowledge and power they need to stay safe while not frightening them or teaching them to mistrust others.

This book is intended to help you meet this challenge. It shows you what you can do to safeguard your children from threats to their physical and emotional well-being. Many institutions such as schools, government agencies, and advocacy groups are making efforts to improve children's safety, but when it comes to your children's safety and protection, you cannot leave it to others. Without question, you are the best person for this job. You are not only the real expert on your children, you are also their most important influence, exerting considerable sway on both their beliefs and their behavior. By using this influence to help your children become more informed and more vigilant, you can give them a greater degree of security and yourself greater peace of mind.

The focus of *Keeping Kids Safe* is on the practical. This is a nuts-and-bolts book offering specific, concrete, and tested strategies you can use to keep your children safe. While a basic premise of this book is as a parent you need to be proactive in order to safeguard your children, I have been mindful of trying to help you teach your children to protect themselves without causing them to be fearful or anxious.

This book addresses eleven issues of concern to parents of children from preschoolers to teenagers. The format is intended to make it optimally useful. Each chapter begins with a brief overview of the issue. The remainder of the chapter outlines essential information, practical suggestions, and proven strategies related to the topic. Each of these expanded lists focuses on what you need to know and do to keep your children safe and secure. Each chapter also contains a list of references providing additional information on the subject as well as a list of organizations that you may wish to contact for further information or assistance.

I want to acknowledge two people who made special contributions to this book. Gloria Fuzia, my editor at Prentice Hall, worked with me from the very beginning to conceptualize this book and help translate the concepts into reality. She was a model of professionalism, lending her keen eye and creative hand to every aspect of this book. I also owe special thanks to my wife, Maxine, for her encouragement as well as her understanding during the many nights I was glued to the computer completing this project.

CHAPTER 1

The ABCs of Finding Safe and Secure Child Care

The birth of their first child brought many exciting moments and new emotions to Kevin's and Rachel's lives, but along with that, they faced the difficult decision of whether they could afford to live on a single income so that Rachel could stay home with their new baby. After many discussions and a thorough review of their finances, they agreed that although it wasn't what they had hoped for, Rachel would have to go back to work.

As a parent you are faced with many difficult and anxiety-provoking decisions. In your child's early years, perhaps no decision causes you more concern than that of entrusting her care to someone else. This issue may give rise to such questions as: Will my child be cared for in the way that I want? Will she be upset and harmed by her separation from me? How will I adjust to being apart from my child? Will my child be safe with her caregiver? These and other issues may preoccupy your thoughts as you go about the process of finding quality child care.

Good child care requires a competent and nurturing caregiver, a safe and comfortable setting, and activities that will help your child grow intellectually, emotionally, and socially. Finding a program that meets these requirements and is affordable and convenient can be a challenge. It is important to put time and

1

effort into finding an arrangement that represents a good fit for your family. Different families have different needs. Whether cost, convenience, or scheduling flexibility is your primary consideration, quality of care is essential and warrants your close attention. A good child care program can shape the way your child thinks, learns, and acts, and thus can lay the groundwork for a successful adjustment to school. Research shows that children in high-quality child care programs make greater strides on measures of intellectual, academic, and social development than children in lower-quality programs. Children who receive inadequate care are less likely to trust teachers and feel secure with their peers upon entering school.

You are the expert on your child and are thus in a good position to choose the kind of care best suited to her needs. To make an informed child care decision, speak with other parents, visit child care programs, and talk with the directors of these programs. While this can be a time-consuming process, it will help ensure that your child receives the best possible care and will more than pay off in peace-of-mind dividends in the long run. It will also lessen the chance that you will need to change child care programs. Adjusting to a new caregiver or program can be stressful for both you and your child.

How your child adjusts in child care depends on more than just the quality of the child care arrangement. The attitude of you and your spouse is also an important variable. Having someone else care for your child may be one of the most difficult adjustments you have to make as a parent. If you feel guilty about having another adult care for your child or if you and your spouse do not agree about putting your child in someone else's care, this can cause stresses that affect the child's adjustment. It is important for you and your spouse to think through the arrangement to make sure that you both support the decision to seek child care. To assist you in this process, the rest of this chapter will provide key information about the many aspects of child care that you should consider. It is intended to help you find the child care option that meets your family's needs and gives you peace of mind.

Some Child Care Facts

- According to a recent survey, 65 percent of mothers with children under the age of six, and 77 percent of mothers of school-age children, are employed.

- Thirteen million children, including 6 million infants and toddlers, are in child care daily.

- Recent national studies have found that at many centers in the United States child care is of poor to mediocre quality.

- A recent University of Colorado survey of child care in four states found only one in seven child care centers to be of good quality.

- While hairdressers and manicurists typically require fifteen hundred hours of training to receive a license, forty states do not require child care providers to have any training in early childhood education.

Making the Child Care Decision

While many parents are required by their family needs to place their child in child care, others have some latitude in making this decision. The following are some factors you might consider in deciding whether to obtain child care for your child:

- Is your child emotionally ready to be in child care?

- Do you expect that the child care arrangement will be a positive experience for your child?

- Do both you and your spouse support the decision to obtain child care?

- How accessible is the child care? How long does it take to get from your home to the child care program, and from the program to work?

- Will the expense of the child care cut substantially into your employment income?

- Do you qualify for local, state, or federal assistance to help you pay for child care?

- How flexible is your employer in allowing you to take time off to deal with any problems related to your child (for example, if she is sick)?

- How available is your spouse if needed during the day?

- Do you have any backup child care if your primary caregiver is unavailable or if your child is sick and cannot attend the child care program?

Child Care Choices

In reviewing child care settings, keep in mind that no option is right for all children. Some children respond better to smaller, more homelike settings while others prefer the excitement of a large center. The following describes the pros and cons of the most common child care options:

NANNY OR AU PAIR: While an expensive arrangement, having someone care for your child in your home allows her to remain in a comfortable, familiar setting and avoids the inconvenience of dropping her off and picking her up. This arrangement may also allow your child to develop a warm, trusting relationship with another adult that is less likely to occur in other child care arrangements. In-home child care is especially beneficial if your child has special needs. To find an in-home caregiver, place an ad in your local paper or find a reputable nanny or au pair agency to help you. Many agencies that screen and train candidates are available. When interviewing candidates, be sure to take the time to ask questions and to communicate your parenting style and values. This will give you an opportunity to get a sense of whether the candidate is one you should consider and if she shares your values. Whenever possible, get referrals from other parents in your area.

IN-HOME SHARED CHILD CARE: In this arrangement two or more families hire a caregiver to take care of a small group of children in the home of one of the families. Some families opt to alternate between homes. This arrangement allows your child to form a close relationship with the child care provider and gives her an opportunity to interact with other children. In considering this arrangement try to find other families that share your child care values, and make sure that the children are compatible.

CARE BY A RELATIVE: Having a family member such as a grandmother or aunt care for your child may be a viable child care arrangement. It would allow your child to be with a caring adult in a familiar and comfortable setting and will likely assure you that she is safe and secure. Bear in mind, however, that your relative may lack the energy and stamina needed to care for a young child. In addition, you may have difficulty being candid with a family member about your child care preferences.

FAMILY CHILD CARE: In this arrangement your child is with other children in the home of a child care provider, often a mother who is also caring for her own child or children. This provides a more flexible, homelike setting than a child care center. A disadvantage is that it may not be regulated by the state, and the caregiver may not be trained in child care. Request proof of licensing and documentation that shows the training the caregiver has undergone, and pay careful attention to safety and health concerns. Also consider your child's compatibility with the other children.

CHILD CARE CENTER OR PRESCHOOL: A child care center usually serves children through the age of five, and a preschool typically offers programs for children from two or three to five years of age. Both are licensed by the state, which sets health and safety standards that the program must meet and may establish staff-child ratios. These programs vary widely in terms of child care philosophy, educational emphasis, facilities, staff-child ratios, admission requirements, and fees. Head Start programs offer free part-time care to children ages three to five from low-income families and to children with disabilities.

No matter which option you choose, it is important that you are encouraged to visit frequently. Take advantage of the opportunity to drop in unannounced. That's when you can discover what the child care environment is like. (If the child care provider comes to your home, make unexpected stops at home.)

How to Find Child Care Options

The sources listed below may either offer child care programs or provide you with information about programs in your community:

- Community organizations
- Churches and synagogues
- Vocational schools and community colleges that offer child care courses
- Head Start programs
- Your employer (some companies offer child care programs)
- Local child care resource and referral agencies
- Local affiliate of National Association for Education of Young Children
- Au pair organizations
- Licensing agency in your state for child care programs
- Better Business Bureau (records any complaints made about a particular center or school)
- Listings in the yellow pages under *child care*, *day care centers*, and *preschool*
- Ads in the local newspaper under *child care*

- Ads in local parenting publications
- Bulletin boards in libraries and retail stores
- Local women's groups
- Your child's pediatrician
- School administrators and teachers
- Word of mouth from other working parents—probably the best source of information

The most important step is a thorough review of potential caregivers. Don't rely on a cute ad for reassurance that the caregiver will be loving and will have your child's interests at heart. Only your most careful scrutiny can ensure that.

How to Determine Which Programs to Visit

While it is essential that you visit a child care program before sending your child there, you will probably not have the time to visit every program in your area. To help you decide which programs merit a visit, you can ask some basic questions over the phone, including the following:

- Where is the center/school located?
- Is the center/school licensed by the state? (Bear in mind that a license only establishes that a center/school meets minimum standards.)
- Are there any openings for children my child's age?
- What is the cost of the program? Is any financial assistance available for low-income families?
- What are the criteria for admission?
- What are the program options?
- Must a child be enrolled for a minimum number of hours weekly?

- How many children attend the program?
- What is the age range of the children in the program?
- What are the hours that the center/school is open?
- On what days is the center/school closed?
- Must children be toilet-trained to attend?

What to Ask the Director of a Child Care Center or Preschool

During your visit to the center/school, be sure to meet with the director to learn what might not be evident from your observations as you tour the program. The following are questions you may want to ask the director. You may find it cumbersome to ask all of them; if so, select those that reflect your values or your particular situation.

- How long has the center/school been in existence?
- Is it accredited by the National Association for the Education of Young Children? (This means the center/school fulfills the standards of this professional organization.)
- What are the application procedures?
- Are siblings of children already attending the center/school given priority when applying?
- Is transportation provided to and from school?
- Are there any extra fees beyond the program cost? Is there a sliding scale?
- Will I be charged for days my child is sick or on vacation?
- Is there a late fee if I am delayed in picking up my child?
- If I decide to remove my child from the program, what are my financial obligations?

- How experienced is the staff in working with children? Are they trained in early childhood education?

- Does the director have experience and training as an early childhood educator?

- Are any staff members trained in first aid or CPR?

- How long have staff members been at the center/school? What is the staff turnover rate? (A high turnover rate means that children often must adjust to new staff.)

- Are the backgrounds of potential employees reviewed for criminal and child abuse offenses? Are references contacted?

- Does the center/school have a written description of its educational philosophy and goals? (If so, ask to review it.)

- Is there a curriculum to be followed by staff? (If so, ask to see it.)

- What is the daily schedule for children my child's age? Is there a rest period?

- Are children grouped? If so, how many children are in each group?

- How many adults are assigned to a group? (Desirable adult-child ratios: no more than three infants per adult; no more than four 1- to 2-year-olds per adult; no more than five $2^{1}/_{2}$- to 5-year-olds per adult.)

- Do children go on field trips in the community? If so, where? How are they transported?

- Do children watch television in the center/school? If so, what programs do they watch? On average, how much time is spent each day watching television?

- What method does the staff use to discipline children?

- How is toilet training handled?

- What kinds of snacks and meals do the children receive? Am I expected to provide my child's lunch or snack?

- What supplies are parents expected to leave at the center/school (such as diapers or items of clothing)?

- Can children bring items from home such as a blanket or a favorite toy to help them feel comfortable and ease their separation from parents?

- Does the staff solicit parent input about their preferences? Are there regularly scheduled parent-staff conferences to discuss the child's adjustment? Is there an opportunity for parents to get weekly or even daily feedback on their children's adjustment?

- Are parents required to participate in the center/school? If so, for how many hours? What activities can parents participate in to fulfill this responsibility? Can they be done during evenings and weekends?

- Does the center/school offer activities for families? Are there workshops for parents about child-rearing and educational issues?

- Can parents visit the center/school at any time?

- Are staff and children required to be immunized?

- What is the center's/school's policy regarding a child attending when he is sick? When is a child considered too sick to attend? How are children who are sick cared for? Are they isolated from the rest of the children?

- What is the policy for contacting parents if their child is sick or upset?

- What is the policy for contacting parents in case of an emergency or a communicable disease?

- What measures are taken to prevent strangers from entering the building?

- What is the policy on releasing children? How do you ensure that only authorized individuals are picking them up?

- Is there an evacuation plan in the event of an emergency?

- Can the director provide names and phone numbers of parents of children attending the center/school to be contacted for references?

What to Look for When Observing a Child Care Program

It is critical that you visit the child care program you are considering for your child. The center or preschool may have an open house for parents. If you are unable to attend, arrange to visit at another time when school is in session (preferably in the morning when children are most active). Be sure to bring your child along when you visit. You can gain important information by watching how she responds to the children and the activities. After the visit, ask her what she liked and did not like about the program. Use the following questions—broken down into the four categories of facility, program, staff, and infant concerns— to guide you during your observations and to ask of the staff when appropriate.

FACILITY/SETTING

- Does the facility appear clean and safe?

- Do the heating, lighting, and ventilation appear adequate?

- Are there smoke detectors and fire extinguishers?

- Are the radiators covered and the heaters protected?

- Are electrical outlets covered with safety caps?

- Are potentially unsafe items such as medications, household cleansers, matches, and sharp items inaccessible to children?

- If the program is located above the first floor, are the windows secured so children cannot climb out?

- Is there a safety plan posted for use in an emergency?

- Are first aid supplies available to staff?

- Is smoking prohibited?

- Is the center/school decorated in a warm, cheerful manner?

- Are the rooms neat and organized?

- Is there enough room for a variety of activities? Can children move around freely and safely?

- Are the bathrooms adequate and easily accessible to children? Do they have a potty chair and a special toilet seat? Is there a step stool to allow toddlers to reach the sink?

- Is there an area where children can nap apart from other children? Is there adequate space for this purpose?

- Is the furniture in good repair and the right size for the children?

- What resources does the program have? Is there a library? Is there a variety of recreational equipment (such as a sandbox, jungle gym, seesaw, swing, glider, and slide)? Does the equipment appear safe?

- Does the center/school have an outdoor area spacious enough to accommodate the children? Is it fenced in? Is it free of litter?

- Are there different indoor activity areas or stations (such as a dramatic play area, an arts and crafts area, a building blocks area, and a reading area)?

- Does the program have a variety of toys such as books, puzzles, beads, blocks, building toys, art materials, dress-up clothes, dolls, trucks, riding toys, pull toys, and wagons? Are there enough toys for the children in the program?

- Are the toys and equipment free of splinters, sharp edges, and points?

- Are materials easily accessible to children?

- Is there a place for children to store personal items?
- Is there a bulletin board to post information for parents?

PROGRAM

- Do the children appear happy and engaged in the activities?
- Do the activities look as if they would appeal to your child? Are they appropriate to her age?
- What kinds of learning activities does the program offer? What does the staff do to stimulate an interest in reading? Are children exposed to age-appropriate activities in the areas of science, music, and art?
- Are there opportunities to learn about different cultures?
- What recreational activities do children engage in on a regular basis?
- Are children discouraged from watching television for long periods?
- Are there opportunities for children to engage in individual as well as group activities?
- Are there teacher-directed activities as well as unstructured play when the children can choose what they want to do?
- Is the work of children displayed? Is it shown at their eye level?
- Are the meals and snacks nutritious? Do mealtimes appear to be pleasant?

STAFF

- Is the teaching or child care staff working and playing with children the majority of the time?
- Is there an adequate number of adults for each group so that children receive sufficient attention?

- Does the staff appear to treat children in a warm, caring, and respectful manner?

- Are there opportunities for the staff to talk with children individually?

- Does the staff make an effort to help children feel important?

- Is the staff sensitive to children who are distressed?

- Do they give support to children who are upset when their parents leave?

- Do they set reasonable limits for children's behavior? Do they explain these limits clearly to the children and reinforce them consistently?

- Are children helped to resolve conflicts with other children in a positive manner?

- Are the children encouraged to be independent and make choices?

- Are they encouraged to explore and make discoveries on their own?

- Does the staff encourage children to ask questions? Do they provide age-appropriate responses in a friendly manner?

- Does the staff pose open-ended questions to children to stimulate and stretch their thinking?

- If a child shows an interest in academic areas such as reading, math, or science, what does the staff do to promote this?

- If a child has a particular interest, what does the staff do to foster this?

- Do children appear adequately supervised when playing outdoors? Can the staff see the entire outdoor area at all times?

- Do staff members offer boys and girls the same encouragement with all activities?

- Do staff members encourage children to engage in healthy practices such as washing their hands and brushing their teeth?

- Do staff members appear to follow good hygiene practices?

PROGRAMS FOR INFANTS AND TODDLERS

- Is the setting arranged so that infants and toddlers can crawl and walk safely?

- Are there safety gates at the top and bottom of stairs?

- Is there a separate play area for infants?

- Do the diapering and toilet areas appear clean and sanitary?

- Is good hygiene practiced with regard to diapering (for example, do staff members wash after every diaper change)?

- Are bottles and food refrigerated?

- Is the staff attentive to the needs of infants when they need to be fed or comforted or have their diaper changed?

- Does the staff make sure that infants are not left alone for long periods?

- Are infants held often (during feedings, for example)?

- Does the staff stimulate infants' awareness by providing things for them to look at, listen to, or touch?

- Does the staff foster children's language skills by talking with them, responding to their verbalizations, naming things, and reading to them?

- Do they seem to enjoy cuddling and playing with infants?

- Do they make an effort to help toddlers learn to feed and dress themselves as well as clean up?

Helping Your Child (and Yourself) Adjust to Child Care

It may take time for your child to adjust to being apart from you and in the care of others. This is a normal occurrence for many children and usually not a reason for concern. At the same time there are some steps you can take to make the transition easier for your child as well as for you.

- If your child is old enough, talk with her about the program a couple of weeks before she begins. Using a calendar, point to the days she will attend the center/school. Let her know how long she will be there and some of the activities she will participate in. Be positive and upbeat when talking about the program.

- Go to the library and get some children's books that sensitively and positively talk about attending child care and read them to your child.

- Visit the program a week or so before your child begins so she can see the setting and meet the staff and some of the children. If she seems particularly friendly with another child, you may want to invite her over for a play date so your child has a friend on the first day she attends the program.

- Consider easing your child into the program by gradually increasing her time at the center/school. A friend or relative may be able to help you out if you cannot pick up your child early.

- Allow extra time to get your child ready the first few mornings she attends the program to avoid the stress of a morning rush.

- Consider having your child bring a comfort item such as a blanket, a favorite toy, or a family picture to the program.

- Spend some time at the center/school during the first few days to help your child feel comfortable. When it is time to leave, say good-bye to her, give her a hug, and leave promptly. She may begin to cry but will likely stop shortly after you leave.

- Give the staff information about your child's siblings, interests, and family pets so they can talk with her about familiar topics and make her feel comfortable.

⊚ Let the staff know about events in your child's life that may affect her mood or behavior. Let them know what they can do to help her if she is upset or uncooperative.

⊚ Make sure the center/school has your work number as well as the number of a relative or friend to call in case of an emergency.

⊚ Set aside time to talk with the staff about how your child's day went. Ask about special accomplishments, interests she has developed, children she is playing with, and problems she is experiencing.

⊚ Leave an extra pair of underwear and pants in a bag with your child's name at the center/school.

⊚ Call if you will be late in picking her up. She may worry or become upset if you are not there at your normal time.

⊚ When you pick up your child, stay for a few minutes to see what she has done, to meet her friends, or to chat with parents or the staff. This way you can show your child your positive feelings about the program.

⊚ Have a child care alternative in case your child is sick and unable to attend the program.

⊚ Build rapport with the staff by volunteering your time for special events.

The Qualities That Matter Most in a Caregiver

In your child's early years one of the most important decisions you may make as a parent is who will care for your child when you and your spouse are at work or enjoying a rare night out. The quality of care your child receives and her safety and well-being will depend on the person providing her care. In seeking potential caregivers, try to find someone who:

- has experience with children your child's age.

- has a good understanding of the needs and abilities of children.

- speaks English well enough to communicate with you and make herself understood to your child.

- has training in child care.

- is sensitive to issues of safety.

- has training in first aid.

- has a good driving record.

- does not smoke in the presence of your child.

- prepares healthy snacks and meals for your child.

- has child-rearing values similar to yours.

- adheres to your wishes regarding the care of your child.

- is respectful of your family's cultural traditions.

- is warm, nurturing, and responsive to your child.

- disciplines your child's inappropriate behavior in a gentle manner, without unnecessary harshness.

- sets out reasonable rules and communicates them clearly to your child.

- does not use physical punishment under any circumstances to discipline your child.

- enjoys teaching and playing with children.

- has a calm, gentle nature and a good sense of humor.

- is patient when helping your child solve problems.

- encourages your child to express herself through language and answers her questions patiently and clearly.

- reads to your child and stimulates her interests.

- encourages your child to explore new activities and engage in creative play.

- encourages independence by allowing your child to do things for herself and learn from her mistakes.

- teaches your child responsibility by encouraging her to pick up after herself.

- helps your child get along with other children.

- does not suggest that certain activities or toys are only for boys or girls.

What to Ask a Potential Caregiver

The interview with a potential caregiver is an important part of the decision-making process. This is an opportunity for you to ask her questions about her background and her child care philosophy, as well as to observe how she interacts with your child. Your child should be present for at least part of the meeting. Keep in mind, however, that your child may be reluctant to interact with someone she's meeting for the first time. Nevertheless, this will give you a chance to see the caregiver's demeanor toward your child. In your interview with her, ask questions that you deem appropriate for your particular situation, such as:

- What experience do you have caring for children? How long have you cared for children, and what were the ages of children you've cared for?

- What was your most recent child care position? Why are you no longer in that position?

- Can you supply references relating to prior child care positions?

- Do you have training in child care? in first aid? in CPR?

- Do you have children of your own? What are their ages? Will your need to care for them interfere with your availability to care for my child?

- Do you have any criminal violations? (For a fee, your state may check to see if an individual has a criminal record.)

- Do you drive? (Be sure to inquire if she has a valid license for your state.) Has your license ever been revoked? (You can check her driving record through your state's motor vehicle agency.)

- Are you willing to drive my child? Do you have a car that you can use to transport her? Does it have air bags? Will you place my child in her car seat and in the rear seat only?

- How is your health? Are you a smoker?

- What do you like about caring for children?

- What do you find difficult or challenging about caring for children?

- What age children do you prefer to care for?

- What kinds of activities would you engage in with my child?

- Will you follow a particular routine with my child?

- Have you ever had to deal with a medical emergency with a child? What happened and how did you handle it?

- How would you handle it if my child swallowed a substance that was possibly poisonous? if she had a high fever? if she began to choke?

- How do you discipline a child who is misbehaving?

- How would you handle it if my child threw a tantrum? if she hit you? if she refused to go to sleep?

- Are you willing to prepare food for my child? What would you do if my child did not like a food you made for her?

- How would you comfort my child if she was upset or angry?

- What will you do with your time when my child is napping? Are you willing to do light housework?

- How long are you available to care for my child?
- When can you begin?

In addition, consider the following:

- Does the person seem open to carrying out your wishes in caring for your child, or does she seem rigid in her child-rearing views?
- Do you enjoy being with this person? Do you feel comfortable talking with her?
- Are you confident that she will treat your child in a kind, caring manner?
- If you're hiring an au pair or live-in nanny, are you comfortable having another person living in your home?

Observe how the caregiver relates with your child and consider the following:

- Is she positive and nurturing with her?
- Does she smile when interacting with her?
- Does she listen attentively to her?
- Does she answer her questions appropriately and in a friendly manner?
- Does she seem to enjoy being with her?
- If your child is quiet and timid, does she seem to understand that this is a normal reaction and not take it personally?

If the caregiver will provide child care for more than one child, consider asking the following:

- How many children will you care for?
- Have you cared for more than one child before? What were their ages?

- What group activities will you do with the children?
- How do you deal with children who are fighting? What strategies do you use to resolve conflicts between them?

What to Ask References About a Potential Caregiver

Before hiring a caregiver for your child, be sure to ask for references and then call them. The following are some questions you might ask:

- How long did she work for you?
- Why is she no longer working for you?
- How happy were you with the care she provided for your child? Would you rate her as below average, average, or above average compared with other caregivers you have had?
- How did she relate to your child? How did your child respond?
- Did your child like her?
- Did she make an effort to adhere to your child-rearing values and preferences?
- Did you have any disagreements with her over child rearing? How were they resolved?
- Was she respectful of your family's cultural traditions?
- Was she responsible about following the schedule that you had established? Did she arrive on time consistently?
- Did you have any concerns about the way she cared for your child?
- Did she have any restrictions or limitations that lessened her effectiveness as a caregiver?
- What kinds of activities did she engage in with your child?

- What approaches did she use in disciplining your child?

- Was she able to calm your child down when she was distressed?

- Did she ever have to deal with a medical emergency? Did she handle it appropriately?

- Did she drive your child? Did you have any concerns about her driving ability?

- If you were looking to hire another child care provider, would you hire her again? Would you recommend her without reservation?

Strategies for Enhancing In-Home Child Care

You can take the following steps to make the child care experience in your home as smooth as possible. These strategies will help ensure that the caregiver meets your child's needs and provides care that is consistent with your values.

- Consider hiring the caregiver a week or so before you return to work. This will give you an opportunity to observe how she relates to your child and to assess her judgment.

- Put in writing the details of the child care arrangement so both you and the caregiver are clear about such matters as salary, work schedule, trial period, holidays, benefits, and arrangements when either the child or caregiver is sick. Also consider placing in the contract how much notice must be given before either you or the caregiver can terminate the employment.

- Discuss with the caregiver the practices that you would like her to follow with your child and what your child is allowed and not allowed to do. You might do this in the presence of your child so she is aware of these rules and knows that the caregiver is expected to follow them.

- If you have a schedule you want the caregiver to follow, write it down and post it in a prominent place.

- Show the caregiver around your home, noting the location of items key to her duties as well as potential problem areas.

- Consider easing your child into the child care arrangement by gradually increasing the time she is with the caregiver.

- Recognize that your child may have some difficulty adjusting to child care; most likely it will take a week or two for her to feel completely at ease.

- Consider asking the caregiver to write down the activities your child engaged in during the day along with any special accomplishments or problems.

- Arrange your schedule so that you allow a few minutes at the beginning or end of the day to talk with the caregiver about your child and care issues. This is an opportunity for you to convey information or make suggestions to the caregiver and for the caregiver to bring any concerns to your attention. Try to do this when your child is not present so you can talk candidly and without interruption.

- Don't hesitate to call home during the day to find out how your child is doing. These calls are an important way to give you peace of mind about your child's care and to discuss any concerns with the caregiver.

- Better yet, occasionally make unannounced visits. This will give you a chance to see the environment your caregiver creates for your child.

- Ask your child periodically about her satisfaction with the child care arrangement, and if necessary, follow up on her concerns.

- Keep the caregiver informed of events in your child's life that may affect her mood or behavior. Let her know what you have found effective in handling these behaviors.

- Have a backup child care provider available in case your primary provider is sick or unavailable.

- Consider paying for child development, child care, first aid, or English classes for an in-home caregiver. Community colleges frequently offer these classes.

- Recognize that the caregiver will occasionally need to take time off to deal with personal matters. Your sympathetic response to these requests will help build trust and rapport with her and promote a more effective child care arrangement.

- If the caregiver lives with you, be respectful of her time off. Avoid asking her to care for your child outside of her scheduled hours or work out a separate fee arrangement.

What to Discuss with a Caregiver

The care your child receives will be best suited to her needs and your preferences if you clearly communicate your expectations to the caregiver. The following are some issues you may want to discuss with her. Some are for caregivers in general, while others are specific to in-home caregivers.

- Your child's special medical needs, including medications and allergies

- Your child's napping and eating schedules

- Strategies for helping your child go to sleep

- Your child's food preferences and any special preparation instructions

- Areas of your home that may present special problems to your child

- The location of important items in your home, including first aid kit, clothes, books, toys, diapers, and videos

- Any special items that may comfort your child such as a doll, stuffed animal, or blanket

- Your preferences in disciplining your child
- Ways of comforting your child when she is upset
- Your preferences regarding toilet-training practices
- The amount of television and the programs your child can watch
- Your rules about having other children over to play
- Your preference regarding whether the caregiver is to drive your child
- Your expectations regarding the caregiver doing housekeeping chores
- Your preference regarding whether the caregiver is to answer the phone or let the answering machine take messages
- Your rules regarding the care of the family pet

Keep This Information on Your Refrigerator

If your child is being cared for in your home, key information such as the following should be posted in a prominent place:

- Your home address and phone number (in case this information needs to be given quickly in an emergency)
- Your work address and phone number
- Your cell phone or pager number
- The following phone numbers:
  - fire and police departments
  - ambulance
  - poison control center
  - your child's pediatrician
  - nearby relative
  - trusted friend or neighbor

⊙ Important medical information about your child, including medications and allergies

⊙ Your child's food preferences

⊙ Your child's schedule

RECOMMENDED READING

Carlton, S., and Myers, C. (1999). *The Nanny Book: The Smart Parent's Guide to Hiring, Firing, and Every Sticky Situation in Between*. Glendale, CA: Griffin Trade Paperback.

Douglas, A. (1998). *The Unofficial Guide to Childcare*. Foster City, CA: IDG Books Worldwide.

Porazzo, K. A. (1999). *The Nanny Kit: Everything You Need to Hire the Right Nanny*. New York: Penguin USA.

Robin, P. (1998). *The Safe Nanny Handbook: Everything You Need to Know to Have Peace of Mind While Your Child Is in Someone Else's Care*. New York: Harper.

Shatoff, D. K. (1998). *In-Home Child Care: A Step-by-Step Guide to Quality, Affordable Care*. St. Louis, MO: Family Careware.

Tabak-Lombardo, E. (1999). *The Caring Parent's Guide to Child Care: Everything You Need to Know About Making Child Care Centers Work for You and Your Child*. New York: Prima.

Van De Zande, I. (1993). *1, 2, 3 . . . The Toddler Years: A Practical Guide for Parents & Caregivers* (2nd ed.). Santa Cruz, CA: Santa Cruz Toddler Care Center.

ORGANIZATIONS

Child Care Action Campaign

330 Seventh Avenue, 14th Floor
New York, NY 10001
1-212-239-0138
www.childcareaction.org

Advocates for quality, affordable child care for all families.

Child Care Aware

1319 F Street, NW, Suite 500
Washington, DC 20004
1-800-424-2246
www.childcareaware.org

> *Provides parents with the name of a child care resource and referral agency that can help them find high-quality child care in their community.*

National Child Care Information Center

243 Church Street, NW, 2nd Floor
Vienna, VA 22180
1-800-616-2242
www.nccic.org

> *This organization's mission is to ensure that all children and families have access to high-quality child care services.*

Parent Watch

49 West 37th Street, 14th Floor
New York, NY 10018
1-800-696-2664
www.parentwatch.com

> *Allows parents to monitor the activities of their children in a preschool or child care center on their home or work computer through video cameras in those settings.*

CHAPTER 2

Lessons in Preventing Violence at School

FEB. 12, 1996—*Moses Lake, Washington. A fourteen-year-old boy walks into a junior high school algebra class with a hunting rifle and opens fire, killing the teacher and two students and wounding another student.*

OCT. 1, 1997—*Pearl, Mississippi. A sixteen-year-old outcast who reportedly worshiped Satan shoots nine students in a high school, killing two of them, including his ex-girlfriend.*

DEC. 1, 1997—*West Paducah, Kentucky. A fourteen-year-old student kills three students and wounds five others while the students are participating in a prayer circle in the hallway of a high school.*

MAR. 24, 1998—*Jonesboro, Arkansas. Two boys, ages eleven and thirteen, open fire from nearby woods on students who have exited a middle school after a false fire alarm. A teacher and four students are killed and ten others are wounded.*

MAY 21, 1998—*Springfield, Oregon. A fifteen-year old student, expelled the day before for bringing a gun to school, kills two students and wounds twenty others in a high school cafeteria.*

APR. 20, 1999—*Littleton, Colorado. Two students, ages seventeen and eighteen, kill fifteen students (including themselves) and one teacher and wound many others at Columbine High School in the nation's most devastating school shooting. The two students had plotted for a year to kill hundreds of students and set off bombs in the school.*

Feb. 29, 2000—*Mount Morris Township, Michigan. A six-year-old boy uses a semiautomatic pistol he brought from home to shoot and kill a six-year-old girl in his first-grade classroom.*

Recent years have brought to the American consciousness a concept virtually unheard of a decade ago: school shootings—violence perpetrated against students by their peers. These tragic events loom large in our memories and remind us that the violence we see all too often in the world has invaded our schools. This violence has not just occurred in inner-city schools. It has also found its way to the suburbs and to rural areas. No geographical region has been excluded, no segment of American society has been spared.

The students and teachers killed and injured in school shootings have not been the only casualties of these senseless murders. The children who attended these schools or watched these events unfold in the media have been victims as well. When students fear they will be targets of violence, anxiety about going to school increases, and concentration while in school decreases. Under these conditions of fear and vulnerability, teachers have difficulty teaching, and students have difficulty learning. Feeling safe and secure in school is a precondition for learning.

While these events are reason for serious concern and warrant our close attention, the fact remains that schools are safe places. Indeed, school crime actually decreased during the 1990s. In 1993 students committed 155 crimes for every one thousand students; in 1997 that figure dropped to 102 crimes for every one thousand students. And school shootings are very rare. Research indicates that children are much more likely to be killed after school, in their own homes, or in their friends' homes than in school.

At the same time, one violent incident is one too many, so schools and communities must take strong and effective steps to prevent school violence. Schools must not only be safe havens for students but also be perceived by students as safe havens. Students must feel safe in school, and parents must feel that their children are safe. Only when schools provide a welcoming climate that is free of intimidation and violence can teachers focus on teaching and students on learning. This chapter describes what you and your school community can do to ensure that your school is safe from violence.

Facts About School Violence

- Violent crime by youth fell to its lowest point in a decade in 1998 and has decreased 30 percent since 1994.

- In the last half of the 1990s, the percentage of high school students who reported bringing a weapon to school declined from 17 percent to 12 percent.

- During a recent school year, 7 percent of schools reported at least one physical attack or fight in which a weapon was used.

- Fights or attacks with a weapon occur most often in middle schools.

- The most frequently reported crime in public schools was physical assault or fighting. In a recent survey, 15 percent of high school students indicated they were involved in a physical fight in school during the previous twelve months.

- Only about 1 percent of gun-related deaths of school-age children occur in or near school.

- More than one in three students—39 percent of middle school students and 36 percent of high school students—report that they do not feel safe at school, according to a recent survey of more than fifteen thousand teenagers.

- Four percent of students recently surveyed stayed home from school at least once in the prior month because of fear for their safety.

- Twenty-eight percent of secondary school students reported feeling left out of activities going on in school.

Factors That May Lead to School Violence

The causes of school violence are difficult to pinpoint and often vary with each incident, but the following factors may help explain why some students engage in violence in school. Typically, more than one factor contributes to a student's violent behavior.

- Easy access to weapons, whether by purchasing them or finding them at home

- Pervasive exposure to violence in popular culture, including movies, television, video games and song lyrics

- Lack of adequate parental supervision

- Use of exceedingly harsh punishment by parents

- Parental hostility toward school authorities, thus reinforcing a child's anger toward school

- Exposure to violence by adults, either in the home or community, conveying the message that violence is an acceptable way of dealing with anger

- Influence of peers or gang members

- Hostility toward people who are different ethnically or racially

- Desire by student to retaliate against those he perceives have mistreated him

- Feelings of low self-esteem

- Chronic academic failure and frustration

- Use of drugs and alcohol

- Community risk factors, including poverty, high unemployment, high crime rate, and physical decline of neighborhood

Warning Signs of the Potential for School Violence

While there is no foolproof method of predicting which students will commit violent acts, this list can serve as an early warning system. The school can then monitor the student closely and perhaps provide him with counseling services. In using this list, be careful about assuming that a student with some of these characteristics will inevitably become violent. Many children have some of them without becoming violent. Obviously, the more characteristics a youngster exhibits, the greater the reason for concern.*

- Has a history of uncontrollable angry outbursts.
- Often engages in name-calling, cursing, or abusive language.
- Makes violent threats when angry.
- Has previously brought a weapon to school.
- Has a history of serious disciplinary problems at school and in the community.
- Has a background of substance abuse.
- Is on the fringe of his peer group and has few or no close friends.
- Is preoccupied with weapons or explosives.
- Displays cruelty to animals.
- Has little supervision or support from parents or a caring adult.

---

* The above list was developed by the National School Safety Center and is printed in adapted form with its permission.

- Has witnessed or been a victim of abuse or neglect at home.
- Has been bullied in school.
- Bullies or intimidates other students.
- Blames others for problems he initiates.
- Consistently prefers TV shows, movies, or music expressing violent themes and actions.
- Prefers reading materials dealing with violent themes, rituals, and abuse.
- Writes essays that reflect anger, frustration, and the dark side of life.
- Is involved with a gang or antisocial group.
- Is often depressed and/or has significant mood swings.
- Has threatened or attempted suicide.

Characteristics of a Safe School

The following list describes desirable school practices that provide the foundation for an effective violence prevention program. While these general educational practices are not specific to school violence, they help deter violent behavior by addressing some of its root causes. Specific strategies for promoting nonviolence as well as school security measures are described later in this chapter.

- Treats students with respect and dignity.
- Has high standards for academic achievement.
- Promotes self-esteem among students by providing opportunities for children of different ability levels and varied interests to succeed.
- Encourages the staff to interact with students in a supportive manner and inform parents about student accomplishments or progress.

- Recognizes students who demonstrate good citizenship or make contributions to their community.

- Offers opportunities for students to get to know and form bonds with teachers.

- Fosters respect and tolerance for students of different backgrounds and abilities.

- Provides a diverse range of after-school activities.

- Offers opportunities for parents to be meaningfully involved in school affairs.

- Has a code of conduct that has been explained to students and distributed to parents.

- Enforces discipline in a consistent and fair manner.

- Has a process for resolving conflicts between students.

- Offers counseling services to students experiencing emotional distress or substance abuse problems or links them with mental health agencies.

- Keeps parents apprised of serious school incidents that might affect students' well-being.

Strategies for Increasing School Security

In recent years schools have implemented a wide variety of ways to improve school security. The following list describes some of them. These strategies may be appropriate for some schools but not others. Schools must be careful to select those that promote enhanced security without unnecessarily alarming or frightening students. It is also important to bear in mind that security measures alone are not sufficient. Sometimes they give schools a false sense of security, and then less attention is given to other needed violence prevention measures.

- Request law enforcement officials or school security professionals to perform a safety assessment of the school.

- Screen prospective staff members for evidence of criminal activity in their backgrounds.

- Create a "safe passage" program in which parents, community members, and businesspeople watch children as they walk to and from school.

- Hire security guards or use parent volunteers or school aides to monitor student behavior inside and outside school.

- Keep only the main school entrance open during school hours and lock all other doors.

- Require that vehicles in the school parking lot have tags identifying them as belonging to the staff, students, or school visitors.

- Mandate that students and staff carry school-issued identification.

- Require visitors to report to the main office, sign in, and carry a visitor's pass.

- Provide school administrators with cell phones that are programmed to dial 911.

- Install metal detectors to identify students carrying weapons.

- Conduct random inspections of student lockers or possessions.

- Require students to put coats in their lockers to lessen their ability to conceal a weapon.

- Permit students to use only mesh or clear backpacks or duffel bags to prevent them from concealing weapons.

- Improve lighting in poorly lit areas of school and grounds.

- Increase monitoring of dark or secluded areas of the school.

- Institute a dress code. Some schools prohibit clothing associated with gangs or require uniforms to decrease disputes related to clothing and jewelry.

- Implement a lockdown drill once or twice a year in which teachers and students lock the doors and windows and go to a designated room.

- Set up offices in schools for probation officers so they can closely monitor students on probation.

- Consider safety issues in designing new school buildings (for example, locate the office centrally for easy access to various parts of the school, eliminate out-of-view stairwells, and place restrooms closer to the main office).

What Parents Can Do to Make Schools Safer

- Contact a school administrator about any safety issues brought to your attention by your child.

- Help supervise routes that students take to and from school.

- Volunteer to be on the school safety committee and participate in the development of the school safety plan.

- Volunteer to monitor the school hallways and patrol the parking lots before and after school.

- Contact the state department of education to gather information on desirable school safety practices.

- Arrange for the principal to make a presentation to the PTA to discuss the school's safety policies.

- Advocate for violence prevention programs at school by speaking to the principal or addressing the board of education.

- Review the school's code of conduct.

- Review school statistics regarding violent incidents at school.

- Conduct an assessment of the school's violence prevention policies, procedures, and programs, using the questions suggested below.

- Request that the school obtain a safety assessment by a school security professional.

- Join or start a parents' organization or chapter to combat school violence, such as Mothers Against Violence in America (MAVIA). (See *Organizations* on page 44.)

Questions to Ask in Assessing a School's Safety Plan

Rather than wondering if your child's school has sound safety guidelines and hoping that it does, request some specific information. Here are some questions you can ask to help you evaluate the safety and security of your child's school.

- Is there a written and comprehensive school safety plan?

- Does this plan reflect input from school administrators, teachers, law enforcement officials, parents, and students?

- Does this plan include a specific and detailed plan for responding to unsafe or violent situations?

- Is there a code of conduct that is explained to students and distributed to parents?

- Does the school give serious attention to student safety concerns and solicit their views about violence prevention?

- Do students perceive the school as safe?

- Do students avoid certain parts of the school because they believe they are unsafe?

- Do students frequently stay home from school because they fear for their safety?

- Are the backgrounds of staff applicants investigated?

- Are teachers informed of serious incidents of school violence?

- Are teachers informed when a troubled or problem-prone student is placed in their class?

- Do teachers and support staff perceive the school as safe?

- Are parents informed of the school's efforts to prevent violence at school?

- Are parents informed of serious incidents of violence at school?

- Is there a system in place for students and parents to anonymously report potentially violent students?

- Does the school have a strict policy about bringing a weapon to school?

- Does the school maintain records on violent incidents and review them to try to detect patterns of school violence?

- Has the school implemented a range of appropriate security measures?

- Do school staff or community members monitor the routes students take to and from school?

- Is access to the school restricted to the main entrance?

- Are school hallways, secluded or poorly lit areas, and the school parking lots monitored by security personnel, school staff, or parent volunteers?

- Has the school improved the lighting in poorly lit areas?

- Has school staff been trained in how to respond to a crisis or a violent incident?

- Does the school employ violence prevention programs such as conflict resolution, peer mediation, multicultural education, and anger management?

- Is there a system in place for identifying troubled or distressed students and referring them to school counselors or mental health agencies?

- Are guidance counselors and psychologists available to meet with students who are troubled or distressed?

- Does the school have a nurse on staff at all times?

Easing Your Child's Concerns About School Violence

Children who are exposed to school violence, either through incidents at their school or reports in the media, may experience distress and anxiety about school. The following steps may guide you in easing your child's concerns about school.

- Monitor his behavior for any signs of distress, including resistance to going to school, difficulty concentrating in class, decline in academic performance, withdrawal from peers, resistance to joining or participating in school activities, and increased dependence on parents.

- Contact your child's teachers to see if they have observed any signs of distress.

- Encourage your child to talk about school and listen to him attentively, especially if he expresses discomfort with some aspect of school.

- Emphasize to your child that he should inform you if he fears for his safety in school and that you will immediately contact a school administrator to try to resolve the problem.

- Acknowledge your child's fears while reassuring him that incidents of violence are rare in school and very unlikely to occur in his school.

- Find out from the school what security measures are being taken to prevent violence and inform your child about these measures.

- If a violent incident has occurred at your child's school, counseling services will likely be made available for students. Encourage your child to talk with a school counselor if he is upset or fearful.

How You Can Promote Nonviolence

To contribute to an environment of nonviolence at your child's school, you can take steps to help your child approach problems in a nonviolent manner. Even if he is showing signs of acting aggressively, you can help curb these tendencies. Just as violence can be learned, so, too, can it be unlearned. This process begins even before a child enters school. You can do the following:

- Make your home a safe, secure place.
- Promote respect for people of different racial or ethnic groups. Model for your child your respect for people of diverse backgrounds. Find opportunities for him to interact with children from different backgrounds.
- Get to know your child's friends and steer him toward good role models.
- Observe how your child relates with other children and encourage considerate behavior.
- Discipline your child without using physical punishment.
- Make it clear, if necessary, that teasing or bullying other children is absolutely unacceptable.
- Review the school's code of conduct and let your child know you expect him to abide by it.
- Set up a reasonable curfew and insist that your child follow it.
- Monitor your child's television watching and video game playing to limit his exposure to violence.
- Talk with your child about the television shows he views. Discuss how in real life people are actually injured by the

violent acts of others. You might ask him questions about the shows such as, "If a person actually did that, what do you think would happen to him?" or "How else might the character have solved the problem without being violent?"

⊙ Encourage your child to participate in after-school activities sponsored either by the school or the community.

⊙ Keep your child from seeing violence in your home or community.

⊙ Communicate strict rules regarding guns and other weapons.

⊙ If you have a gun in your home, consider removing it.

⊙ If you keep a gun in your home, take every precaution to ensure that it is not accessible to your child. Bullets should be stored separately from the gun, and both should be locked away securely.

⊙ Solve conflicts at home in a reasonable, nonconfrontational manner. This will model good problem-solving skills for your child.

⊙ Talk to your child about the consequences of violent behavior.

⊙ Teach your child some strategies for dealing with anger and frustration. These can include the following:

  – Talk to yourself and tell yourself to calm down.
  – Take a few deep breaths.
  – Imagine a pleasant scene.
  – Think about the consequences of acting on your anger.
  – Count backwards from ten to one.
  – Resolve to deal with the problem later when you are calmer.
  – Talk with a guidance counselor at school.

What Students Can Do to Make Their School Safe

- Alert a school administrator if you suspect a student is dangerous.

- Immediately report any crime to a school administrator or the police.

- Inform a school administrator or your guidance counselor if you have knowledge that a student is considering suicide.

- Make students who are new to the school feel welcome.

- Initiate a "peace pledge" in which students promise to resolve disputes nonviolently and to promote a safe school.

- Become a peer counselor or mediator and help other students resolve conflicts nonviolently.

- Serve on a teen court.

- Serve as a mentor to a younger student who is experiencing behavioral problems in school or shows the potential for violence.

- Start or join a student patrol or school crime watch, perhaps through the Youth Crime Watch of America. (See *Organizations* on page 44.)

- Start or join an antiviolence program such as Students Against Violence Everywhere (S.A.V.E.). (See *Organizations* on page 44.)

- Encourage student groups to adopt an antiviolence theme.

RECOMMENDED READING

Blauvelt, P. D. (1999). *Making Schools Safe for Students: Creating a Proactive School Safety Plan.* Thousand Oaks, CA: Corwin Press.

Boelts, M. (1997). *A Kid's Guide to Staying Safe at School.* New York: PowerKids Press, Rosen Publishing Group.

Giggins, P. O. (1997). *50 Ways to a Safer World: Everyday Actions You Can Take to Prevent Violence in Neighborhoods, Schools and Communities.* Seattle, WA: Seal Press.

Newton, D. E. (1995). *Teen Violence: Out of Control.* Springfield, NJ: Enslow Publishers (for young adults).

Quarles, C. L. (2000). *Staying Safe at School: What You Need to Know.* Nashville, TN: Broadman & Holman Publishers.

Saunders, C. S., and Espeland, P. (1994). *Safe at School: Awareness and Action for Parents of Kids Grades K–12.* Minneapolis, MN: Free Spirit Publishing.

Schleifer, J. (1994). *Everything You Need to Know About Weapons in School and at Home.* New York: Rosen Publishing Group.

ORGANIZATIONS

Mothers Against Violence in America (MAVIA) and Students Against Violence Everywhere (S.A.V.E.)

105 14th Avenue, Suite 2A
Seattle, WA 98122
1-800-897-7697
www.mavia.org

MAVIA works to reduce violence by and against children through education and advocacy. S.A.V.E. is a MAVIA program open to students who want to change attitudes and behaviors that contribute to violence.

National Resource Center for Safe Schools

101 SW Main, Suite 500
Portland, OR 97204
1-800-268-2275
www.safetyzone.org

A comprehensive resource on issues related to keeping students safe in schools.

National School Safety Center

141 Duesenberg Drive, Suite 11
Westlake Village, CA 91362
1-805-373-9977
www.nssc1.org

Created by a presidential directive with the mandate to promote safe schools through training in violence prevention.

Ribbon of Promise National Campaign to End School Violence

150 Seventh Street
Springfield, OR 97477
1-541-726-0512
www.ribbonofpromise.org

Educates the public on matters related to school violence.

Youth Crime Watch of America

9300 South Dadeland Boulevard, Suite 100
Miami, FL 33156
1-305-670-2409
www.ycwa.org

A youth-led organization that works to create a crime- and drug-free environment in schools and neighborhoods.

CHAPTER 3

Keeping Your Child Safe After School

"It's 3:00 P.M. Do you know where your children are?"

Like many parents you may consider this more than a public service announcement. This question and all that it implies may be one that you have to grapple with in trying to balance your own work demands with your child's needs. Figuring out how to provide your child with positive and productive activities after school while keeping her safe and secure can be a major issue.

In recent years there has been a large increase in the number of dual-career and single-parent families. Add to this the decrease in extended family available to help with child care, and it becomes clear that parents must rely on outside sources more than ever when it comes to caring for children in the after-school hours. While many parents have found good after-school programs for their children, others have chosen self care—that is, they allow their children to stay home after school while they are at work. A recent survey indicates that approximately one of every seven American children between the ages of five and twelve spends time without adult supervision after school.

Having children in self care is not a recent occurrence. During World War II when large numbers of women worked in defense plants and there were few child care options, many children were left home alone in the after-school hours. They came to be known as latchkey children, a term often used today, because they wore their house key on a string around their neck.

Some children thrive on being in self care. They may take pride in being allowed to be on their own, relish the freedom of self care, and easily manage the responsibility while experiencing little anxiety. Being on their own may also boost their self-esteem and confidence. Others may not fare as well. They may be anxious, lonely, or bored, and may comfort themselves by watching television, eating junk food, and doing little else. Older children who are expected to supervise their younger siblings after school may be overwhelmed by the responsibility or frustrated from missing out on after-school activities. Children who are unsupervised after school and spend time with peers outside of the house are even more likely to run into problems than children who stay home alone. This is especially true of adolescents, who may become involved in antisocial activities, substance abuse, sexual activity, or criminal mischief.

In this chapter various issues relating to the after-school hours will be discussed, including the options available to working parents, evaluating after-school programs, factors to consider in deciding on self care, precautions to take if a child is home alone before or after school, and bus safety. Some careful planning can go a long way toward avoiding problems.

After-School Alternatives for Working Parents

To obtain after-school alternatives that meet their needs as well as those of their children, working parents have a number of options. Which option to choose depends on many factors, including the appropriateness of the option for your child, the cost, the availability of transportation, and scheduling considerations. The primary options are listed below.

In-Home Child Care. While this may be more expensive than other after-school arrangements, having a caregiver in your home offers consistency and flexibility. It allows your child to have friends over the house, and the caregiver may be able to take her to and from after-school activities or to friends' houses. You may want to consider sharing this arrangement with another family to help defray the cost of the sitter.

Child Care in Another Home. This alternative may also allow your child to go to after-school activities or have play dates with friends. The school district may be willing to have the school bus drop her off at a stop near the caregiver's home if it is on the route.

After-School Cooperative. You and other parents might organize an after-school child care program, with each member responsible for child care on a rotating basis

School-Based Child Care. This option has the advantage of allowing your child to remain in a familiar setting that is designed for children, and usually with children she knows. However, the program may not be compatible with your schedule if you need to pick up your child late.

Self Care. Having your child stay home alone after school may be a viable choice for you. Much of this chapter is devoted to discussing how to help your child be safe and secure if you opt for self care.

Combined Program. While difficult to arrange, you may want to use a combination of after-school options. (For example, your child can stay with a sitter three days a week and go to a recreational program two days a week.)

Community-Based Program. Community organizations, such as the recreation department, the local "Y," or a Boys & Girls Club, may run after-school programs.

Job-Based Child Care. More and more companies are offering on-site child care. If not available at your place of work, you may want to consider advocating for this alternative.

WORK FLEXTIME HOURS. Some companies allow employees to stagger their hours so they can be more available to their children after school.

WORK PART-TIME. By restricting your work schedule to when your child is in school, you can be available to her after school.

WORK OUT OF YOUR HOME. More and more parents are opting for this alternative, although many find it difficult to get work done when their children come home from school.

What to Look for in an After-School Program

After-school programs differ greatly in the training and experience of their staff, their range of activities, and their facilities and equipment. Take some time to examine the various programs by visiting them, talking with the staff, and observing the children and the activities. Ask yourself whether the program is a good match for your child and her interests. A well-run program matched to your child's needs can help develop her self-esteem, promote friendships and social skills, bolster academic skills, and foster new interests and skills. The following are some of the questions you might want to consider as you review the program options:

- Does the facility appear clean and safe? Is it decorated in a warm, cheerful manner? Is there enough room for a variety of activities? Are the restrooms adequate?

- What resources does the program have? Is there a library? Is there sports equipment?

- Is there a favorable staff-to-child ratio?

- How experienced are the staff in working with children? What is their background?

- Does the staff treat the children in a respectful and caring manner?

- Do the activities look interesting to your child? Are they appropriate to her age and skill levels? Do the children in the program appear to be having fun?

- Are children taken on field trips and, if so, where do they go?

- Are there opportunities for children to participate in community service projects?

- Are children given time to do homework? Are staff members available to help with homework or provide tutoring? Will the staff talk with your child's teacher to coordinate instruction?

- Are learning or enrichment activities (such as story time) part of the program?

- Are children encouraged to develop self care skills?

- Are nutritional snacks provided?

- Are staff members available and willing to discuss any concerns you may have?

- Are children required to attend every day or can they attend fewer than five days a week? Is the program open before school and on holidays? How late can children stay there? Is there a late fee if you are delayed picking up your child?

- Is transportation from your child's school to the program provided (or from the program to school if she attends before school)?

- What is the cost of the program? Are there any extra fees?

Issues to Consider in Deciding on Self Care

In deciding whether to have your child stay home alone, consider the following:

- Any legal restrictions in your state about when a child can be left unattended (check with your state's child welfare agency)
- The safety of your neighborhood
- The amount of time your child will be home alone each day
- Her comfort level while home alone
- Her maturity level and ability to solve problems
- Her willingness to comply with your rules when she is home alone
- Your availability by phone
- Her ability to communicate with adults by phone
- The availability of a nearby adult in case of emergency
- Your employer's cooperation in allowing you to talk with your child daily and, if necessary, leave work in the event of an emergency
- Any medical condition that your child has that demands special care or attention
- If more than one child is staying home unsupervised, the ability of your children to get along
- Any stress your older child may feel from having to supervise a sibling

Is Your Child Ready to Be Left Alone?

There is no simple formula for deciding whether your child is ready for self care, nor is there a particular age when she should be considered ready. In making this decision, her chronological age is less important than her maturity level. A general rule of thumb is that a child should be at least twelve before she can care for herself, and at least fifteen before she can be responsible for a sibling. Some very responsible and mature children may be ready before these ages, although some parenting experts maintain that parents should not leave a child under the age of ten alone for an extended period no matter how mature. The following list should help you assess your child's readiness for being home alone and identify areas where she needs some guidance. While you do not need to answer "yes" to every one of the following questions to consider her ready to be home alone, the more "yeses" you can answer, the more confident you can feel that she is ready for self care.

- Can your child lock and unlock the door?
- Can she lock and unlock the windows?
- Can she tell time?
- Can your child get herself a snack?
- Does your child know how to use the phone?
- Does she know her address, phone number, your and your spouse's names, your places of employment, your work numbers, and the nearest cross street to your home?
- Does she know how to call you at work?
- Does she know how to call the operator?
- Is your child comfortable answering the phone?
- Does she know not to tell callers that her parents are not home?
- Can your child write a message?
- Can she read instructions that you have left?
- Has your child shown that she can follow your directions?
- Can you rely on your child to follow the rules you have established?
- Does she know your rules regarding having friends over the house after school?
- Does your child know not to allow strangers in the house?

- Has your child been comfortable when she has been in situations where an adult was not present?

- Is your child comfortable staying home alone?

- Is she comfortable being home alone during a storm?

- Has your child shown the ability to solve minor problems when an adult was not present?

- Has she shown good judgment when she has had to make decisions on her own?

- Does your child know whom to contact if there is a problem and you are unavailable?

- Do you have confidence that she will make the right decisions in case of an emergency?

- Does your child know to call 911 or other numbers in the event of an emergency? Does she know what to say? Does she know not to hang up until told to do so?

- Does she know the quickest way to leave the house in case of fire?

- Does she know where the first aid kit is?

- Does she know what to do for a nosebleed, burn, bruise, or a minor scrape or cut?

- Does she know what to do if the electricity goes out? Does she know where a flashlight is?

- If you have more than one child staying home unsupervised after school, are you confident they can get along reasonably well and resolve conflicts on their own?

- If you are planning to have an older child care for a younger sibling at home after school, do you think she can handle this responsibility without feeling much stress?

- If you are considering having your child care for herself in the morning, is she able to get herself ready in the morning and leave for school on time?

Preparing Your Child for Self Care

The time that your child is home alone can seem like an eternity to you if you are not confident she will be safe and secure. According to one survey, employee accidents and mistakes are more likely around 3:00 P.M. when children are due home from school and working parents may be worried about whether their children arrived home safely. The following suggestions will help you prepare your child for being home alone and give you peace of mind.

- Ease your child into self care. Consider a trial run: Have her stay alone for a short time while you do an errand. Talk with her afterward about how she felt. If she is comfortable, gradually increase the time she is left alone.

- Choose a set place where your child will keep her key, such as in a zippered part of her backpack. Have her attach it to something that is easy to find, such as a shoelace. You might tie or sew the shoelace to an inside part of her backpack so there is little chance of losing it.

- Consider giving a key to a trusted neighbor in case your child loses hers, and let your child know that the neighbor has a spare. If the neighbor with the key is not home, your child should know to go to another neighbor's house (tell her which neighbor) to call you.

- Make sure your child can answer the phone and make calls on her own. If she needs help, unplug the phone and practice with her.

- Set up a check-in procedure. Make an arrangement with your child that either you will call her or she will call you when she gets home. If you are to call her, consider getting a watch with an alarm to alert you when to call. If she is to call you, instruct your coworkers to put your child through or, if necessary, track you down. If you are not available by

phone, consider getting a pager or having your child check
in with a neighbor.

- Provide nutritious snacks for your child that require little or
  no preparation.

- Instruct her in kitchen safety, including which knives, if any,
  she can use; wiping up water spilled on the floor; turning
  the handle of a pot toward the back of the stove or avoiding
  use of the stove altogether; and using a stepstool rather than
  a wobbly chair or the counter to get something.

- Find other adults your child knows who will be available to
  her in person or by phone if there is a problem and you are
  unavailable. Have at least two people she can call in case one
  is not home, and let them know that your child may be calling if there is a problem.

- If you can find transportation, try to arrange for her to be involved in after-school activities once or twice a week.

- If your child has activities after school, be sure to discuss the
  plans in the morning, paying particular attention to transportation issues.

- Make arrangements in advance about what your child
  should do if school closes early.

- Let your child know when you will be home and when
  you're going to be late. Even small delays can be a source of
  worry to children home alone.

- Do a safety check of your home. (In some communities a
  member of the police department will do this for you.)
  Make sure your child has no access to firearms, liquor, or
  matches, and eliminate any items that could be dangerous,
  such as chemicals and flammable materials. Repair potential
  hazards (for example, frayed wires) and check that smoke
  alarms, the furnace, the water heater, and appliances are
  working properly.

- Have a fire extinguisher in your home and show your child how and under what circumstances to use it.

- Teach her what to do if her clothes catch on fire: stop, drop, and roll.

- Cut the bushes near your home so nobody can hide behind them.

- If you live in a high-crime area, consider establishing a "safety room" in your house. Tell your child to go a specific room or closet in the event that burglars or strangers enter the house. You might have a cordless phone, some emergency numbers, and, if necessary, a flashlight in this area.

- Make certain there is a first aid kit in the house containing iodine, first aid cream, bandages, adhesive tape, gauze pads, scissors, calamine lotion, and an icepack. Show your child where it is kept and how to use the various items for basic problems.

- Post emergency numbers as well as your address next to the phone (see pages 60–61).

- Role-play with your child situations that may occur when she is home alone by asking her some "What would you do if . . . ?" questions. While you don't want to frighten her with these questions (reassure her that many of these situations are unlikely), rehearsing these situations may help her feel more confident and in control. The following are examples of situations you may want to role-play:

  - Having someone stop her on the way home to ask if she wants a ride home
  - Getting a phone call for a parent
  - Having a stranger come to the door
  - Dealing with a friend who wants to come over when your rule is that friends are not allowed over without adult supervision

- Calling an emergency number and knowing what to say, including her address and phone number

- Handling hot food from the microwave (if she is allowed to use it)

◌ Check whether your community offers a course in "survival skills" for children in self care and enroll your child.

◌ Let your child know that you want her to tell you if she has any worries about being home alone even if they seem minor. Concerns about seemingly minor issues may mask a greater discomfort about being home alone. Check with her periodically about how things are going. While she may initially welcome the chance to stay home alone, she may become anxious and fearful. Take her concerns seriously and make adjustments to ease her worries. If she appears continually fearful about staying home alone, you may want to adjust your schedule or get a sitter.

◌ Consider getting a dog. It can be a comfort to a child who is home alone and the barking may scare off intruders.

◌ You may want to leave a taped message for your child to listen to when she gets home with suggestions about snacks, activities, or chores. Just the sound of your voice can be comforting.

◌ If you have more than one child at home after school and you anticipate that they will have conflicts, rather than having your older child be responsible for the younger one, consider giving each child some responsibilities.

Some Basic Rules for the Latchkey Child

It is important that you set out clear rules for your child to follow while she is home alone. Safety concerns should be paramount. However, don't feel as if you must have a rule for every possible situation, or you may overwhelm or frighten your child.

Tell her only as much as she can handle for her age. Write the rules down clearly and briefly, post them in a prominent place, and occasionally review them with her. The following suggested rules for latchkey children can be adapted to conform to your values and your child's maturity level.

- She is to keep her house key hidden from view and not show it to others, so as to avoid inviting trouble by publicizing her home-alone status.

- She is to go home directly after school and is not allowed to stop over a friend's house unless she gets permission from you in advance.

- She is not to have friends over the house after school unless she has obtained permission from you beforehand.

- She is not to enter the house if she sees or hears something unusual (for example, the door is open, a window is broken, there are strange people in the house, or she hears unusual noises). If so, she is to go to a neighbor's house and inform her of what she observed so the neighbor can respond appropriately.

- She is to keep the door locked at all times and not open it for any reason. She should not go to the door or a window so as to give the impression that no one is home.

- If she receives a phone call for a parent, she is to tell the caller that her parents are busy and not available to come to the phone. If necessary, give your child a precise message to tell the caller (for example, "My mom is busy and can't come to the phone"). She is not to give her name or the family's name to any caller. As an alternative, she can let an answering machine record calls unless they are from people she knows.

- She is to hang up the phone if she gets a call and hears strange noises or upsetting comments. Have her tell you if this happens and let her know that the person isn't calling her but is randomly picking numbers to call. Consider changing your number if it becomes an ongoing problem.

- If she feels nervous or frightened, she is to call you. If you are not available, she is to call an adult that you have designated. In an emergency she is to call 911.

- In case of fire she is to leave the house as fast as possible with any siblings (show her the quickest way out), go to a neighbor's house, and ask the neighbor to call 911. Emphasize that she is not to stop to get any items or go back in to retrieve anything. If you live in an apartment building, tell her to use the stairs rather than the elevator.

- If you have more than one child staying home, they are to settle minor disagreements on their own without any hitting. Any unresolved problems can be discussed when you get home.

- Depending on your child's age and maturity level, consider establishing rules or limits in the following areas: television watching, computer use, foods that she is allowed to eat and not eat, homework, places she is allowed to go outside of the house, use of kitchen appliances and tools, and caring for pets.

Important Phone Numbers to Post at Home

If your child is home alone after school, post the numbers listed below next to the phone. You might get a phone that can be programmed to dial a number at the press of a button. Show your child how to use this feature and practice with her if necessary. You might also post your address and phone number next to the phone in case she needs to give this information in an emergency. Even if your child knows your address and phone number, in an emergency she may not be able to recall them.

- Your work number
- Your cell phone number
- Your pager number

○ The numbers of two nearby adults

○ The number of a relative

○ Fire department

○ Police department

○ Ambulance

○ Poison control

After-School Activities for Latchkey Children

Your child may settle into an after-school routine of watching television and doing little else. While watching some television after school is understandable, encourage other activities. Sit down with your child and together come up with a list of alternate activities, using the suggestions below as a starting point.

○ Arts and crafts projects

○ Games and puzzles

○ Reading a book or magazine (have her choose one or two magazines to subscribe to)

○ Working on a collection

○ Practicing a musical instrument

○ Writing a story

○ Making a special snack

○ Homework

○ Chores

○ Play date with a friend

○ After-school activity in school or community

○ Community service

Some activities may require that you prevail on a friend or neighbor to transport your child. If so, find ways of reciprocating when your schedule permits.

When Your Child Is Home Alone Before School

Your schedule may require that you leave for work before your child leaves for school. If she is on her own in the morning, consider taking the following steps to help her get off to school without problems:

- Establish a morning procedure. Talk with her about what she must do before leaving the house, including preparing breakfast, getting her lunch or lunch money, placing homework in her backpack, locking the door, turning off the lights and any appliances, and if necessary, operating the alarm. You might post a brief list of these tasks in a prominent place.

- Take care of school business the night before. Mornings will be less frantic for you and your child if you get certain tasks done the night before, such as checking homework, making sure all school materials are in her backpack, making lunch or giving her lunch money, laying out her clothes, and filling out forms and signing permission slips. Set up a box with money that your child can take from if you forget to give her lunch money.

- Set an alarm to go off five minutes before your child must leave for school or call her from work. Children home alone in the morning are not always reliable about leaving for school on time.

- Arrange to have a friend pick up your child in the morning. This may also help ensure that she leaves for school on time.

- Plan in advance what your child should do if she misses the school bus. Tell her whether she is to go to a specific neighbor's house and ask for a ride or come home and call you.

How to Enhance School Bus Safety

The school bus is a safe means of transportation, but accidents with school buses can and do happen. Every year, some nine thousand children are injured and thirty-five are killed in school bus accidents. Most of these accidents happen when children are outside of the bus and hit by a passing vehicle or the school bus itself. You can protect your child by taking some of the following precautions, depending on your child's age and experience.

- Make sure your child has a book bag or backpack for her papers so that loose papers do not blow away on the bus.

- If it is dark when your child walks to or from the school bus, have her wear bright clothing to increase her visibility.

- Instruct your child in the following school bus rules in accordance with her age:
  - Stand back as the bus approaches and do not walk toward the bus until it comes to a full stop.
  - Go to your seat immediately and stay seated until the bus stops and you are ready to get off.
  - Buckle the seat belt (if available).
  - Do not put your hands or head out the window.
  - Do not yell or talk loudly while on the bus.
  - Do not carry glass items on the bus.
  - Move away from the bus after getting off and wait for the bus driver to tell you to cross the street.
  - Always walk at least ten feet in front of the bus when crossing so you are visible to the bus driver.

– Do not go back to pick up an item you dropped until the bus driver has clearly directed you to or the bus has left.

In addition, use the following guidelines to help your child feel comfortable and confident in riding the school bus.

⊙ Introduce yourself and your child to the bus driver. Knowing the bus driver will help your child feel more comfortable and will be an advantage in resolving bus problems.

⊙ Make sure your child knows where to wait for the bus and where to get off. Walk a young child to and from the bus stop at least the first few times. Drive the bus route with her from school to home and point out her bus stop so she knows where to get off.

⊙ Avoid having your child get to the bus stop too early to minimize the potential for problems.

⊙ Have your child memorize the number of her school bus so that she does not get on the wrong one. Tell her to ask the driver if she is not sure it is the right bus.

⊙ Try to find a child in your neighborhood with whom she can sit on the bus.

Precautions to Take if Your Child Walks to School

If your child walks to and from school, the following tips will help you encourage her budding independence while keeping her safe.

⊙ Walk or ride from your home to school and choose the safest route for your child, avoiding danger spots such as empty lots, alleys, and wooded areas. Point out to her safe places to go in an emergency such as a neighbor's house or a store. Instruct her to take the same route every day.

⊙ If necessary, teach your child how to cross the street. Emphasize the following:

- Follow the crossing guard's instructions.
- Cross at the corner.
- Keep within the crosswalk.
- Look both ways before crossing.
- Watch for cars turning the corner.
- Be alert for bikes.
- At a traffic light cross when the light facing you is green or the "walk" sign is on.
- Do not walk into the street between parked cars.

- Arrange for your child to walk to school with a friend.

- Give your child a whistle to alert others if she feels she is in danger, or instruct her to yell if she is approached by a stranger

- Let your child know that she can call 911 from pay phones.

- Do not have your child wear clothes with her name in a place that others can see.

- If your child is fearful of meeting up with certain peers on the way to school, find another route to take or ask the school principal to talk with students who may be bothering your child.

- If your child thinks she is being followed, instruct her to go quickly to a place where there are other people, such as the school, a store, or a neighbor's house.

- Instruct your child to avoid anyone she doesn't know who approaches her. Tell her not to accept rides or items offered by anyone unless she has your permission in advance, and not to respond to anyone's questions. Make it clear that you will *always* let her know in advance if someone other than you is picking her up and that she is not to accept a ride under any other circumstances.

- Make sure she knows not to hitchhike.

- If your child rides a bike to school, insist that she wear a helmet.

- Arrange a code word with your child to be used by a person unfamiliar to your child whom you have asked to pick her up.

- Make sure the school has a way of contacting you if your child does not show up at school.

Using the Public Library As an After-School Alternative

Some parents arrange for their children to stay at the public library after school while they are at work. Some libraries have even arranged for children to be transported from school to the library after school. The following suggestions may help make your child's use of the library more enjoyable and problem-free:

- Talk with the librarian to find out if the library has any policy about children staying there after school without adult supervision.

- Introduce your child to the librarian and inform her that she will be at the library after school.

- Keep in mind that the librarian will not be available to supervise your child.

- Take your child on a tour of the library and show her where the bathroom is.

- Teach her how to use the library's resources, including its card catalog or online system for locating books, and make sure she has a current library card.

- Establish basic rules for your child to follow while at the library. Emphasize the importance of being quiet and considerate of others.

- Find out if the library offers any after-school programs or activities for children such as story hour, clubs, films, arts and crafts projects, or instruction in home-safety skills.

- Consider whether your child needs to bring a snack to eat in the library. Ask the librarian if this is permitted.

- Plan with your child what she should do if you are late picking her up and the library has closed.

What Communities Can Do to Help Latchkey Children

Working parents need the help of their communities in ensuring that their children are safe and secure after school. The following are some steps that schools and communities can take to provide support to working parents and their children:

- Offer a parent-alert program in school in which volunteers call parents if their child has not arrived at school.

- Establish a safe-house program identifying safe places children can go before or after school in the event of an emergency.

- Hold a fair for parents featuring various after-school programs.

- Offer after-school activities at the public library.

- Assign a librarian to be responsible for children who attend the library after school on a regular basis. Some city libraries have recruited adult volunteers to be at the library to help students with homework.

- Offer after-school programs in the schools or other community settings.

- Provide transportation from school to after-school programs or the public library.

○ Offer a course to latchkey children in self care skills, including neighborhood safety, home and kitchen safety, first aid, safe telephone practices, self care when sick, caring for siblings, and nutrition.

○ Begin a telephone hotline (often called "phone friends" or a "warm line") that unsupervised children can call to obtain guidance and support. This can be helpful when parents are not accessible by phone.

○ Provide a homework hotline for children who need assistance with school assignments.

RECOMMENDED READING

Books for Kids

Bunting, E. (1990). *Is Anybody There?* New York: Harper Collins.

Gray, N. (1992). *I'll Take You to Mrs. Cole.* Brooklyn, NY: Kane/Miller.

Stewart, M. M. (1993). *Ellen Is Home Alone.* New York: Skylark Books.

Books for Parents

Bergman, A. B., and Greene, W. (1995). *The Complete School-Age Child Care Resource Kit.* West Nyack, NY: Center for Applied Research in Education.

Grollman, E. A., and Sweder, G. L. (1994). *Teaching Your Child to Be Home Alone.* Lanham, MD: Lexington Books.

Long, T. J., Buchanan, C. D., and Paul, P. (1985). *Safe at Home, Safe Alone.* Alexandria, VA: Miles River Press.

MacGregor, C. (1999). *365 After-School Activities You Can Do with Your Child.* Holbrook, MA: Adams Media Corporation.

ORGANIZATIONS

"Grandma, Please!"

Senior Services, Jane Addams Hull House
501 West Surf
Chicago, IL 60657
1-773-525-0395
www.hullhouse.org

A Chicago-based after-school reassurance line for latchkey children who need to talk to an adult. The volunteers, typically senior citizens, provide support, friendship, and encouragement to the children who call. Other communities have similar programs for children who are home alone and want to talk to someone; these are often called Phone Friends programs. If you are interested in creating such a program in your community, call 1-773-525-0395.

National Institute on Out-of-School Time

Center for Research on Women
Wellesley College
106 Central Street
Wellesley, MA 02481
1-781-283-2547
www.wellesley.edu/WCW/CRW/SAC

Works to ensure that all children, youths, and families have access to high-quality programs during off-school hours.

National Safe Kids Campaign

1301 Pennsylvania Avenue, NW, Suite 1000
Washington, DC 20004
1-202-662-0600
www.safekids.org

Works to educate the public about how to prevent unintentional injuries to children.

The following companies offer after-school educational centers that provide academic programs for students. Go to the websites or call the numbers below to find a center near you.

Huntington Learning Centers

www.huntingtonlearning.com
1-800-692-8400

Score! Educational Centers

www.scorelearning.com
1-888-eSCORE4

Sylvan Learning Centers

www.educate.com
1-800-338-2283

CHAPTER 4

Helping Your Child Handle Bullies and Peer Pressure

Matthew has always been a bright student, with a lot of enthusiasm for school. He always had many friends and got along well with his classmates. Ever since entering middle school, though, his parents have seen a change in his behavior. He has been making a lot of negative remarks about school, and his demeanor in the morning is a far cry from his sunny disposition of the not-too-distant past.

His parents were troubled by the change in Matthew's attitude toward school, but decided it was part of an inevitable adjustment period that most students entering middle school experience. What they didn't know was that what Matthew had to adjust to was more than a new school and a more challenging academic workload. Instead, it was Joe, the biggest kid in the class, maybe even in the school, who had decided that Matthew was a perfect target for his abuse. It seemed as if Joe never passed up an opportunity to establish his physical superiority over Matthew. He harassed him at the bus stop, jostled him in the hallways, tripped him in the cafeteria, and taunted him in every way possible. Although other students observed these incidents, they did not report them to school staff, nor did any staff members seem to notice them. Throughout the ordeal Matthew suffered in silence, fearful of antagonizing his tormentor. His behavior, however, spoke volumes about the effects of the bullying. Matthew's schoolwork declined dramatically, he became unusually anxious and withdrawn, and he began resisting going to school.

71

Although it may be of little comfort to Matthew, he is in good company. He is one of many students who are bullied every day at school. Most of us can probably recall incidents of bullying from our own school days, but we need to realize that bullying is a pervasive problem in our schools—and one of the most serious. Being taunted or attacked physically can be a painful ordeal, one that leaves lasting psychological scars. Victims may experience anxiety, depression, and low self-esteem, often leading to a reluctance to go to school. Further, its impact extends beyond the victim. Bullying can engender a climate of fear and anxiety that distracts students from their schoolwork.

A recent survey indicated that because of bullying about 10 percent of students are afraid during much of the school day. But despite the widespread and serious nature of bullying, schools do not always give it the attention it deserves. While some schools may not act because they are unaware of the behavior, others may not act even after hearing reports of bullying. They may take the view that "boys will be boys" and that students have to learn to stand up for themselves. Yet students should not be left to fend for themselves in the face of bigger and stronger students who are aggressive and harassing.

Bullying makes children feel unsafe, and when they feel unsafe in school, it can dominate their lives both in and out of school. Students need to know that schools will take the problem of bullying seriously and that they will be protected. Further, they need to feel comfortable letting a parent know when they are the target of a bully. If principals, teachers, and parents place the safety and security of children at the top of their priority list, the school bully can be dealt with in a way that ensures his victims' safety and preserves a healthy learning environment for all students.

To help you protect your child if he ever becomes the target of the school bully, this chapter provides information about what you and your child can do to deal with the problem of bullying. In addition, this chapter discusses another kind of peer problem: peer pressure. While this issue may be less intimidating to children than bullying is, it is no less of a concern to parents. Peer pressure stems from the desire and need many children have to gain the acceptance and approval of their peers, which may lead some to engage in risky behaviors.

Some Surprising Facts About Bullying

- Bullying is one of the most serious and pervasive problems in our schools. Surveys indicate that 15 to 20 percent of all students are victimized by bullies at some point in their school career.

- The National Association of School Psychologists estimates that 160,000 children miss school every day for fear of being bullied.

- Most incidents of bullying take place in or around schools, particularly in areas with minimal supervision such as the playground, rest rooms, locker room, cafeteria, and hallways.

- Bullies are often very adept at keeping staff from noticing their harassment of other students.

- Most incidents of bullying go unnoticed. Even when teachers notice them, they do not always take action. According to a recent survey of students, 71 percent of teachers or other adults in the classroom ignore bullying incidents.

- Victims of bullying often fail to report incidents to school staff because they are not confident the school will take their concerns seriously or take steps to curb the problem. They may also avoid informing staff because of shame about what happened or fear of retaliation.

- Bullying starts in elementary school, reaches its peak in middle school, and gradually declines in high school. By high school bullies and victims are often pursuing different interests and subjects in school so their paths are less likely to cross than in middle school.

Myths About Bullying

You may hear people make statements that downplay the seriousness of bullying. They are often false or misleading. Be careful that you do not fall into the trap of perpetuating these myths, including the following:

"BEING BULLIED BUILDS CHARACTER." Rather than building character, being bullied can damage a child's self-esteem and cause him to be anxious, fearful, and unhappy. He may come to believe that something is wrong with him. Some people contend that bullying can be a learning experience, but for most victims the only thing they learn is that the world is unsafe and people are not to be trusted. These are hardly healthy lessons.

"BULLYING IS A HARMLESS RITE OF PASSAGE. IT'S PART OF GROWING UP." While bullying is a fact of life for many children, this does not mean it is a natural part of childhood. And it is certainly not harmless. Bullying can often leave lasting psychological scars. In fact, research suggests that many children consider being bullied the worst experience they can have with the exception of the death of someone close to them.

"THAT'S NOT BULLYING. IT'S KIDS BEING KIDS." Bullying is far different from kids fooling around. When children engage in horseplay, they do so out of choice. Victims of bullying do not choose to be tormented. And bullies and victims are not on an equal footing. Typically there is an imbalance of power, with a stronger, physically imposing student intimidating a weak or vulnerable one.

"STICKS AND STONES MAY BREAK YOUR BONES BUT NAMES CAN NEVER HURT YOU." In an effort to help their young child deal with teasing, some parents recite this familiar saying. But it is of little comfort to a child who is constantly being teased or called names. The scars left by verbal attacks, especially if they are frequent and ongoing, can often last longer than those from physical blows.

"What Did You Do to Make Him Act That Way to You?" Asking the victim this question is equivalent to pinning the blame on him. We need to convey the opposite message to victims—namely, that they did nothing wrong and it is the bullies who have the problem. Bullies often choose their victims for arbitrary reasons—because they have a different skin color, an accent, a speech impediment, or because they wear the wrong clothes, have big ears, or are short—so it is important for your child to know that he didn't do anything to provoke the bully and that it is not his fault.

"He Just Has to Learn to Stand Up for Himself." While children need to learn to resolve conflicts with their peers, this does not mean they should be left to fend for themselves in the face of extreme aggression. Some students are simply unable to deal with intimidation from often bigger and stronger students. In these cases they need the help of an adult, and it needs to be explained to them that seeking help is not a sign of weakness, but rather a sign of good sense.

"Hit the Bully Back, and He Won't Bother You Again." In most cases this will only make the situation worse. Bullies usually prey on victims smaller and weaker than themselves, so retaliating could result in the victim's getting hurt. Also, encouraging your child to strike back is giving him the message that violence is acceptable.

"I Was Bullied When I Was in School, and I Turned Out Fine." While some children weather bullying more easily than others, many experience long-term pain as a result. And those who claim that they survived the ordeal may have forgotten the genuine hurt they felt at the time.

"No Kids Are Bullied in This School." Don't believe it. While some principals would like you to believe that bullying is nonexistent in their schools, the reality is that virtually every school has bullies.

A Profile of Bullies

Children who bully others may have the following characteristics:

- Typically, it is boys who bully, although girls may also engage in aggressive or abusive behavior toward their classmates.

- Are typically bigger and stronger than their peers.

- Have a history of aggression toward other children going back to early elementary school.

- Have a need to be in control and dominate their peers.

- Feel no sense of remorse at hurting another child.

- Are unpopular with their classmates.

- Tend to perceive hostility where none is present.

- Tend to lash out at classmates with little provocation.

- Lack the social skills to resolve conflicts through cooperative means.

- Are frequently defiant of authority figures.

- Are prone to academic difficulties.

- Often come from homes where there is little parental supervision and a lack of warmth and attention.

- Are taught from an early age that might makes right, that the way to get what they want is through force.

- Are more likely than their peers to have problems later, including dropping out of school, having difficulty holding jobs, being abusive of their spouses, and having aggressive children.

Bullies often grow up to be harsh, punitive parents who have children who also become bullies.

A Profile of Victims

Children who are taunted or bullied by their peers tend to display the following characteristics:

- Are weaker than their tormentors
- Have low self-esteem and confidence
- Have poor social skills
- Have difficulty making friends
- Tend to be isolated from their peers
- Have problems standing up for or defending themselves
- Become easily upset or are prone to crying
- Tend to be sensitive and insecure
- Are overly dependent on others
- Are prone to picking on younger students as a way of venting their frustration

How Bullies Use Aggression

Bullying can take many forms. Most bullying is verbal. Male bullies are more likely to attack others physically or verbally, while female bullies are more likely to harass others through indirect social means, such as excluding peers or spreading rumors about them. Bullies show aggression toward other children in such ways as:

- Teasing or taunting
- Making sexually or racially offensive comments
- Writing nasty things about them
- Intimidating or threatening
- Hitting, pushing, kicking, or pinching

- Taking or damaging belongings
- Stealing or extorting money
- Getting them in trouble
- Spreading rumors
- Persuading their peers to reject or shun them
- Making them do things they do not want to do
- Having unwanted physical contact with them (in situations where boys bully girls)

Why Children Bully

Bullies may engage in aggressive behavior for a variety of reasons. They may intimidate or harass their peers as a result of their own negative experiences or to achieve certain effects such as power or status. The reasons are many and complex, and can include any number of the following:

- Gaining a sense of power and control over peers by making them fearful
- Boosting their status, influence, and popularity with other children
- Venting frustration with problems at home. Bullies are frequently the products of unhappy home environments or parents who are harsh or punitive and provide the child with little warmth and positive attention.
- Venting frustration with problems in school
- Taking out their anger on others because they have been bullied themselves.
- Punishing a child of whom they are jealous
- Having been manipulated into acting aggressively by friends

- Having been exposed to violence in the media, with the message that aggressive behavior is "cool"

Whatever the reason, bullying needs to be stopped as soon as it is observed.

Is Your Child Being Bullied?

Your child probably won't tell you that another child is bothering him, so you will need to be on the alert for clues from his behavior that something is amiss. In particular, you may have reason for concern if your child:

- is fearful about attending school.
- is scared of walking to or from school or riding the school bus.
- often develops a stomachache or headache in the morning.
- comes home from school with torn clothes.
- has unexplained cuts or bruises.
- is unusually hungry after school (due to his lunch money being stolen).
- is missing some of his possessions.
- frequently asks for or takes money (which he may need to give to a bully in school).
- experiences a decline in his academic performance.
- seems isolated from his peers.
- has become moody and quick to anger.
- is withdrawn, depressed, or tearful when he comes home from school.
- has begun to act aggressively toward other children.
- has problems sleeping or eating.
- talks of or attempts suicide.

Helping Your Child Deal with Bullying

Few things make parents more upset than hearing that their child is being bullied. Some may react by telling him that he has to stand up to the bully. Others may want to protect him by confronting the bully or his parents. Neither approach is likely to improve the situation. Some ways to help your child cope with a bully include the following:

- Encourage him to let you know if another child is bothering him, and assure him that he is not tattling.

- If you see signs that your child is upset about something, ask him if another child is bothering him. Keep in mind that he may be embarrassed to tell you that he is being bullied or may fear you will take action that will antagonize the bully and make the situation worse.

- If your child says another child has been bothering him, take his concern seriously. Listen attentively and let him know he did the right thing by telling you. Do not lead him to believe you will keep the information secret, but reassure him that he will not have to face the problem alone and you will help resolve it.

- Reassure your child that he is not to blame for the bullying. Be careful not to suggest that he may have done something wrong. Let him know that it is the bully who is acting inappropriately, not him.

- If your child is different from his peers (for example, if his first language is not English) and this difference has led to negative comments, let him know that every child is different in some way and help him take pride in this difference. A proud, confident child is less likely to be targeted by a bully.

- Help your child counter negative comments with positive ones (such as, "When Sean calls me stupid, it's because he wants other kids to think he's cool. But he's the one with the problem, not me. My grades are a lot better than his anyway").

- If your child has been a target of bullies in a number of settings, ask yourself what it is about him that is drawing their attention. (Does he stand alone during recess? Does he cry easily? Does he wear unfashionable clothes? Does he pick his nose?) Then try to help him change his behavior in a way that does not suggest to him that he did anything wrong.

- Have your child describe to you precisely what happened and then brainstorm with him some ways of avoiding contact with the bully. (The section on page 83 offers some ideas for doing this.)

- Role-play with your child encounters with the bully. You play the role of the bully and have your child try out responses. Encourage him to use assertive behaviors where appropriate, such as saying "no" in a firm manner to another child's demands and then walking away. Examples of responses are listed later in this chapter.

- Consider talking with the bully's parents. Keep in mind, however, that they may be uncooperative or defensive about their child. If so, avoid a confrontation with them and look for other ways to resolve the problem.

- If your child is being bullied in school, keep a record of dates and names of those involved, and schedule a meeting with his teacher as soon as possible. Alert her to what he has told you and elicit her observations. Help develop a plan of action for the school to follow, which may include talking with the offending student or contacting his parents. This may require the involvement of the principal if, for example, more supervision is needed on the playground. When you get home, write a letter to the teacher thanking her for her support and summarizing the steps to be taken. Check back with the teacher after a few days to find out if the situation has improved.

- Do not overreact to your child's report of bullying by storming into school and angrily demanding action. You may damage your relationship with school officials, whose cooperation might be needed to resolve the problem.

- If your child is being taunted on the bus, let the principal or bus driver know so he can monitor the situation. Suggest that children be assigned seats and that the bully be placed far away from your child.

- If your child is being bullied on the way to or from school, consider driving him or having him walk with older children.

- Suggest to your child's teacher that she find ways to highlight your child's accomplishments in class to help give him some status among his peers. Let her know about his particular talents and interests.

- Help your child develop friendships. The more involved he is with other children, the less he will be a target for bullies. Find some social activities that he may be interested in joining. Also, encourage him to invite children over to your home. Invite one child at a time so there is no chance that your child will be "odd man out."

- If you find that the school is not taking your child's complaint seriously, consider taking him to his doctor and getting a letter from the physician documenting his distress and the importance of the school's taking immediate action to relieve the problem.

- Monitor the situation closely. Ask your child often how things are going. If the bullying is continuing, take additional steps.

- Keep a record of incidents that your child describes to you. Also keep copies of letters you have written regarding the bullying and a record of those to whom you have spoken.

Helping Your Child Avoid Being Bullied

Sometimes the best way to deal with a bully is to figure out how to prevent incidents. While it is not fair for your child to go out of his way to avoid contact with a bully, making these changes may spare him some distress and anxiety. Here are some avoidance strategies you can suggest:

- Sit near the bus driver on the school bus.

- Take a different route to or from school or leave a little earlier to avoid meeting up with the bully.

- Do not bring expensive items or a lot of money to school.

- If you are being harassed in the hallway, try taking a different route to your classes.

- Avoid unsupervised areas of the school and situations where you are isolated from your classmates.

- Make sure you are not alone in the locker room.

- As a last resort, request a change of schedule or, better yet, insist that the bully's schedule be changed.

Tips for Your Child on Dealing with a Bully

Children being victimized by bullies may feel helpless, but they can take a number of steps to protect themselves, including the following:

- Tell your parents so they can advise you on how to deal with the bully.

- If the incident happens in school, seek help from your teacher, guidance counselor, or principal. If you are not comfortable doing this on your own, take along a friend or ask your parent to do it.

- Do not retaliate against the bully or get in an angry exchange with him. This may make him even more determined to torment you. Instead, consider a response that is likely to defuse the situation.

- Respond simply and firmly to the bully or else say nothing and then walk away. A bully thrives on upsetting another child because it gives him a feeling of power, so don't let him see that he has hurt you. He may get bored when he is ignored or does not get the response he wants.

- If you sense the bully may hurt you if you don't give him what he wants, opt for safety and meet his demands. It is not worth getting hurt over a possession that can be replaced.

- Establish friendships with other children. A bully is more likely to leave you alone if you are with a group of friends, especially if they will stick up for you.

- Project a confident air. Rather than hanging your head and seeming downcast, stand straight, hold your head high, make eye contact with others, and walk with confidence. If you can do this, the bully will be less likely to single you out.

What Your Child Should Say to a Bully

When faced with a bully's taunts, your normally bright and articulate child may find himself completely tongue-tied, conveying even more weakness to his victimizer. Help him prepare some ready responses. They do not need to be lengthy, clever, or funny. Have your child practice these responses at home and remind him to speak confidently while looking the bully in the eye. This way the bully may sense that your child is not as vulnerable as he thought. The following are some examples:

- Say "no" in a firm manner and then walk away.

- If the bully takes something of yours or does something you do not like, use a direct and concise "I" message such as "That's my book and I need it back."

- Hold your ground if a child tries to take something of yours by saying something like "You can't have this ball. John and I are playing with it."

- Ask the bully to repeat what he said: "Could you tell me that again?" This may take the wind out of his sails.

- Tell the bully, "You know something? You're right," and then walk away.

- Ask the bully an assertive question, such as "What's your problem?"

- Say something unpredictable that throws the bully off-stride, for example, "I'll bet you can't say that five times fast."

- Respond to the bully's taunts with something short and simple, such as "That's your opinion" or "Whatever you say." Then walk away.

- Try a conciliatory approach: "I don't want to argue with you. Do you want to play a game with me?"

- Use humor to disarm the bully: "That's the nicest thing anybody's ever said to me."

- Appeal to the bully's desire for peer approval: "Teasing kids is a pretty nerdy thing to do."

How Your Child Can Help a Victim of Bullying

If your child sees someone being bullied, tell him not to join in and encourage him to try to help. Doing nothing is saying that it is okay to bully others. Although your child shouldn't place himself at risk, you might suggest that he take the following steps:

- Refuse to join in if the bully tries to recruit you in his efforts to torment someone.

- If you are confident the bully won't turn on you, consider telling him to stop what he is doing by saying something like this: "John, leave him alone. He didn't do anything wrong. We don't like the way you're treating him." This is especially effective if you can get other children to give him the same message.

- Try to distract the bully by getting him to focus on something else.

- Suggest to the child being bullied that he talk with his parents or teacher. Tell him that you will go with him to speak with the teacher.

- If he is unwilling to talk with someone, consider telling an adult yourself, but without letting the bully know so that he doesn't become aggressive toward you.

Bully-Proofing Your Child's School

Bullying in schools is not just a problem for its victims, it makes all students feel unsafe. Schools must make it clear that student safety is an essential part of their mission by sending a strong message that bullying will not be tolerated and enlisting the support of the students. To accomplish this schools can do the following:

PROMOTE A CLIMATE OF COOPERATION AND CARING. Schools can help deter bullying by encouraging acts of kindness and communicating values of cooperation and tolerance. Of course, the most effective way to foster a caring attitude in school is for school staff to model this behavior.

SURVEY THE SCHOOL ABOUT BULLYING. A survey of students, teachers, and parents may reveal how pervasive bullying is in the school. It may also indicate when and where students are being harassed.

ESTABLISH A CLEAR ANTIBULLYING POLICY. Make sure this policy is clearly communicated to staff, students, and parents.

EMPOWER THE SILENT MAJORITY TO TAKE ACTION. Because the staff is not always present when bullying takes place, schools need to encourage students to report any incidents. This might be done at a schoolwide assembly. Tell students that reporting bullying is not the same as tattling on a student. Help them understand what it feels like to be teased and taunted, and make it clear that they are not to join in when they observe a child being bullied.

MAKE IT SAFE FOR STUDENTS TO REPORT BULLYING. School personnel must keep the names of students who report bullying anonymous. Until students feel confident that this will happen, bullying will go unreported and bullies will continue to thrive. The school might set up a box in classrooms or the main office where children can leave notes about incidents of bullying.

BE ALERT FOR SIGNS THAT A STUDENT IS BEING BULLIED. Possible indicators of bullying include a student's reluctance to come to school, his avoidance of school areas such as the playground, withdrawal from peers, unusual fearfulness or anxiety, difficulty focusing in class, and a decline in grades.

TAKE REPORTS ABOUT BULLYING SERIOUSLY AND ACT QUICKLY. Schools should follow up on all reports of bullying. Putting an immediate end to one child's hurting another is vital not only to protect the student but also to send a message to other students that bullying will not be tolerated.

COACH STUDENTS BEING TEASED ON HOW TO RESPOND. Teachers and guidance counselors may want to help a student being teased learn how to be assertive without being aggressive. A student being victimized by a bully needs to learn how to deflect the bully's taunting without provoking him or appearing upset.

DISCIPLINE STUDENTS WHO BULLY. The purpose should be to deter the bully's aggressive behavior rather than to humiliate or embarrass him. In addition to insisting that the bully return any items taken from the victim, the principal might exclude him from places or activities where he has harassed other students.

CONTACT THE PARENTS OF THE BULLY. The school should consider meeting with the bully's parents to inform them of his actions and gain their support for changing his behavior. The student should be apprised of the school's course of action and be informed that his parents support the plan.

TRY TO CONNECT WITH THE BULLY RATHER THAN CONTROL HIM. Talk with the student in a nonthreatening manner, listening attentively without condoning his behavior. Try to find out what triggered his actions. It may be that he wrongly perceived hostility from the other student. Talk with him about how his behavior will cause classmates to avoid him out of fear. Ask him how else he might have responded and offer some suggestions of your own.

USE PEERS TO HELP VULNERABLE STUDENTS. Schools may create programs in which students assist vulnerable peers. They may help orient new students, mediate peer conflicts, and befriend students who are rejected by peers. Older children may be assigned to help younger students who are being bullied.

PROVIDE CLOSE SUPERVISION OF AREAS WHERE BULLYING IS LIKELY. Bullying often takes place in relatively unsupervised areas such as the bus stop, rest room, locker room, hallway, cafeteria, stairwell, and playground. Students who fear being bullied may avoid these areas.

ATTEND TO THE VICTIM EVEN AFTER THE BULLYING ENDS. Check with the student periodically. Even if the bullying has stopped, the school may still want to provide him with guidance, particularly if he is isolated from his peers. His teacher or guidance counselor may want to help him develop friendships and learn how to assert himself if other children are bothering him.

MONITOR THE BULLY'S BEHAVIOR. If he continues to bully other students despite concerted efforts by school personnel to change his behavior, consideration should be given to removing him from his class or even the school. The victim's program should not be changed to avoid coming into contact with the bully.

What You Need to Know About Peer Pressure

- Peers play a large role in the life of a teenager, typically replacing family as the most important social force in his life. Increasingly he looks to peers for support, believing they are better able than his parents to provide understanding and sympathy.

- Adolescents, who are grappling with figuring out who they are while also establishing some independence from their parents, find comfort in belonging to a peer group that decides for them how to think and act. Being accepted by their peers is a paramount concern for teens and may dominate their thinking. Conformity is at its peak as they strive to look, talk, and act like their classmates.

- In their desire to gain peer approval, preteens and teenagers typically feel pressure to engage in the activities of their peers. Sometimes they will succumb to this pressure against their better judgment. Children with low self-esteem are particularly vulnerable to this pressure and may lose their perspective about right and wrong.

- Coping with peer pressure is one of the toughest parts of growing up. These pressures are most intense during a child's middle and high school years. Children with nurturing parents are more likely to resist peer group values that differ from their family's values and are thus better able to resist negative peer pressures.

- Peer pressure does not necessarily lead children astray; indeed, it can be a force for good if it encourages them to engage in healthy, productive activities such as joining athletic teams, working hard in school, and doing community service. It can also help children develop a sense of right and wrong.

Helping Your Child Cope with Peer Pressure

Standing up to peer pressure is one of the greatest challenges that children face. Many are unable to stand up to the challenge and are led into participating in risky or even illegal activities. Help your child deal with peer pressures by doing the following:

STRENGTHEN THE BOND WITH YOUR CHILD. He will be more likely to respect your views and values and better able to resist peer pressure if he has a good relationship with you and feels you are a source of support. This bond needs to be nurtured long before your child's teenage years.

PROMOTE YOUR CHILD'S SELF-ESTEEM. Children who are confident and have positive self-worth are more likely to pursue friendships with children who are good role models and better able to resist negative peer pressure. Find opportunities to boost your child's self-esteem and enjoy success by involving him in activities that capitalize on his strengths and interests. And, of course, praise him for things he does well at home.

SET A GOOD EXAMPLE. Your child is a keen observer of what you do and may learn more from what he sees than what he hears. If he sees that you are constantly striving to keep up with other parents, he will likely do the same with his peers. If he sees you drinking and smoking, he is less likely to resist engaging in these behaviors. If you do drink or smoke, giving it up will make a vivid impression on him.

TALK WITH YOUR CHILD ABOUT PEER PRESSURE. Let your child know that you understand how hard it can be at his age to do things that make him stand out. Tell him that his peers may respect his decision not to join them in an activity even though they may not express it, and that some may even admire his courage in resisting what they could not. Help him understand that a friend who is pressuring him to do something that may be harmful is not much of a friend. Appeal to his desire for autonomy by encouraging him not to let others manipulate or make decisions for him.

AVOID OVERREACTING WHEN TALKING ABOUT PEER ISSUES. Your child may tell you things that may make your jaw drop. If you overreact, you will discourage him from talking with you about these issues again. At the same time use these teachable moments to introduce some cautions without moralizing or lecturing. Although it may seem as though he is dismissing what you are saying, he will hear you.

CHOOSE YOUR BATTLES CAREFULLY. Don't make an issue out of your child's wanting to wear the same clothes as his friends or adopt a trendy hairstyle. Make your stand on high-risk peer behavior. Battling your child constantly over minor issues may drive your child toward peers who are similarly alienated from their parents. Not sweating the small stuff will enable you to be more effective when you challenge him on the larger issues.

HELP YOUR CHILD DEVELOP GOOD DECISION-MAKING SKILLS. If he can learn to trust his own instincts when making decisions, he will be less likely to let others make decisions for him. Encourage him to think through the possible consequences of the decision he is facing, including whether it may cause him harm. Let him know that giving in to the pressure now may make life harder for him later on.

HELP YOUR CHILD DEVELOP RESPONSES TO PEERS. Help him figure out what to say to peers who are pressuring him to participate in high-risk activities. Suggest responses that are short and simple and that he can say comfortably. If he is receptive, role-play with him or encourage him to practice in front of a mirror.

GET TO KNOW YOUR CHILD'S FRIENDS. Make a point of encouraging your child to invite his friends home. Spend some time with them and assess whether they are positive influences.

DON'T HESITATE TO SET LIMITS FOR YOUR CHILD. Your willingness to say no to him sets a good example and may help give him the courage to say no to a peer when faced with a potentially harmful situation.

SET LIMITS ON YOUR CHILD'S OUT-OF-SCHOOL WORK SCHEDULE. He may feel pressure to make money to buy clothes, CDs, and magazines to keep up with his peers, yet working excessive hours can cause him to fall behind on his schoolwork and give rise to unnecessary stress.

How You Can Promote Positive Peer Relationships

Friends are all-important to adolescents. No matter how confident a child is and how strong his bond with his parents, he will inevitably seek the support and approval of his peers. So rather than trying to lessen the influence of his peers, recognize that this is a fact of teenage life and put your efforts into trying to foster positive relationships with other children.

ENCOURAGE YOUR CHILD TO BECOME INVOLVED IN ORGANIZED ACTIVITIES THAT REFLECT HIS INTERESTS AND STRENGTHS. These activities, whether in or out of school, are good opportunities for him to meet children who are positive influences and have similar interests. In addition, he will be less drawn to negative peer activities if he has appealing alternatives.

ORGANIZE ACTIVITIES FOR YOUR CHILD AND HIS FRIENDS. Encourage your child to have friends over the house when you are there to supervise. Suggest some activities they can do and, if they allow you, join in with them. In this way you can exercise some control over how they spend their time.

PROMOTE YOUR CHILD'S RELATIONSHIP WITH GOOD ROLE MODELS. Have your child invite a friend whom you perceive to be a positive influence to a special outing, such as a movie, a dinner out with the family, or a sporting event. This may help to strengthen their friendship.

GET TO KNOW THE PARENTS OF YOUR CHILD'S FRIENDS. By forging a relationship with parents of children who are positive role models, you can help solidify your child's connection with these children. In addition, you and the other parents can establish similar ground rules over such issues as curfews. If your child's peers have to follow rules similar to those you set, it will make your child less likely to challenge your restrictions.

RECOMMENDED READING

Books for Kids

Johnston, M. (1998). *Dealing with Bullying.* Center City, MN: Hazelden (grades K-4).

Romain, T. (1997). *Bullies Are a Pain in the Brain.* Minneapolis, MN: Free Spirit Publishing (ages 9-12).

Romain, T. (1998). *Cliques, Phonies, and Other Baloney.* Minneapolis, MN: Free Spirit Publishing (ages 9-12).

Scott, S. (1997). *How to Say No and Keep Your Friends: Peer Pressure Reversal for Teens and Preteens* (2nd ed.). Amherst, MA: Human Resource Development Press (preteens and teens).

Books for Parents

Alexander, J. (1998). *Bullying: Practical and Easy-to-Follow Advice.* New York: Penguin Putnam.

Fried, S., and Fried, P. (1996). *Bullies & Victims: Helping Your Child Through the Schoolyard Battlefield.* New York: M. Evans.

McCoy, E. (1997). *What to Do When Kids Are Mean to Your Child.* New York: Penguin Putnam.

McNamara, B., and McNamara, F. (1997). *Keys to Dealing with Bullies.* Hauppauge, NY: Barron's Educational Series.

Zarzour, K. (2000). *Facing the Schoolyard Bully: How to Raise an Assertive Child in an Aggressive World* (2nd ed.). Buffalo, NY: Firefly Books.

ORGANIZATIONS

Conflict Resolution in Education Network

1527 New Hampshire Avenue, NW
Washington, DC 20036
1-202-667-9700
www.crenet.org

Committed to creating safe schools by making conflict resolution education an integral part of the educational program of all schools.

National Association of School Psychologists

4340 East West Highway, Suite 402
Bethesda, MD 20814
1-301-657-0270
www.naspweb.org

Promotes educationally and psychologically healthy environments for children and youths by implementing programs that prevent problems, enhance independence, and foster learning.

CHAPTER 5

Protecting Your Child from the Lure of Gangs

Gangs used to be viewed as an inner-city problem, plaguing low-income families and their communities. But inner-city residents don't have a monopoly on dysfunctional families and chaotic lives. Families from all social classes and all walks of life can share the common bond of troubled homes. As a result, children from any social class can become susceptible to the lure of gang life.

Gangs can have a far-reaching impact on their members, the families of these members, and the communities in which they live. Youths who join gangs often become immersed in the gang's activities. In extreme circumstances the gang replaces their family, and former friends are cast aside. Members may go to extreme lengths to defend the gang's honor and to prove their loyalty, including the use of violence. Being in a gang poses many risks to its members, including the very real risks of physical injury and a criminal record.

Families of gang members can suffer as a result of a family member's gang affiliation just as gang members themselves can. Parents may have to deal with the emotional and financial burdens of a child frequently in trouble with the law as well as the fear that their child or another family member could be a victim of gang violence. And the gang can cause fear, intimidation, financial hardships, and a poor quality of life for members of the community.

What You Should Know About Gangs

A gang is a group of individuals who regularly associate with one another and typically engage in antisocial, violent, or criminal behavior. Gangs often have a formal organizational structure with a leader and members that have specific roles and responsibilities. Here is additional information about gangs:

- A 1998 survey by the National Youth Gang Center indicated that there are approximately 28,700 gangs in this country with nearly eight hundred thousand active members.

- The vast majority of gang members—about 90 percent—are male, although female gang membership has increased in recent years.

- Gang members are typically between the ages of twelve and twenty-four. Gangs often target children for membership, knowing they will receive lesser penalties than older members if caught engaging in a crime.

- While gang members tend to come from low socioeconomic strata, youth from all social and economic backgrounds have been known to join gangs.

- Although they tend to be organized along racial and ethnic lines, about one third of gangs have members from more than one ethnic or racial group.

- Many gang members are high school dropouts and have few employable skills.

- A disproportionate number of gang members are illiterate.

- Members typically express their loyalty by wearing the gang's style and color of clothing, using gang slang, and flashing specific hand signs.

- Members may advertise their gang identity by writing the gang's name and symbols on their personal belongings.

- Gangs tend to be identified with specific neighborhoods and often use graffiti to mark their territory. Rival gang members who enter another gang's territory are targets for attack.

- Gang members commit serious and violent offenses far more often than adolescents who are not in gangs. Gangs may engage in a variety of criminal activities, including vandalism, extortion, arson, robbery, car theft, and selling drugs.

- Gangs have become more violent in recent years largely because of access to and use of increasingly lethal weapons.

Types of Gangs

The following are some of the types of youth gangs that can be found in communities across the nation. A gang may fall into more than one of the categories listed below.

TERRITORIAL GANG. This type attempts to exert control over a certain area, often using intimidation and violence to protect its turf.

ENTREPRENEURIAL GANG. Its overriding goal is to make money, and although the "entrepreneurial" label may suggest ingenuity and productivity, illegal means are often used, most often selling drugs. Violence is a routine part of this group's activities.

HATE GANG. Members direct their hatred and violence toward select groups, usually of a racial or ethnic nature. Skinheads and white supremacists are examples of this type of gang. Their message of hatred may be reinforced with an extreme political ideology advocating societal change. For example, white hate gangs may advocate the elimination of all programs to advance minorities.

ETHNIC OR RACIAL GANG. The members of this gang share the same ethnic or racial heritage and typically live in the same neighborhood; they thereby obtain a sense of belonging and identity that they do not feel in the larger society.

How Gangs Recruit Members

Gangs maintain their power and influence by recruiting new members. They do this in any of the following ways:

LURE OF THE GANG. They promise power, money, sex, and the chance to "be somebody." Their visual symbols, including hand signs, graffiti, tattoos, and distinctive clothing, appeal to many young people, particularly those with few or no other interests to occupy their time or those seeking a sense of belonging and satisfaction.

DECEPTION. They misrepresent the true nature of the gang, leading new members to believe they are joining a social group or club. They may tell them they need to join a group to protect themselves against potential enemies. Gangs may also target vulnerable children, offering the caring and support they are not getting at home.

OBLIGATION. Gang members may do a favor for a potential recruit (for example, providing money or protection) and then demand that he join the gang as payment for the favor.

INTIMIDATION. Threats or force are often used to coerce youths into joining.

PEER PRESSURE. A potential member may be led to believe he will be a "nobody" if he does not belong to a gang.

SELF-RECRUITMENT. Some youths may find a gang attractive and become friendly with gang members in the hopes of joining.

Why Youths Join Gangs

Here are some of the reasons that youths might join a gang:

TO GAIN A SENSE OF BELONGING AND IDENTITY. Being in a gang may give youths the sense of belonging and being part of a family that they do not get in their own home. It may also provide them with support, acceptance, and companionship from their peers. As a result, their loyalties may switch from family members to gang members.

TO GAIN POWER AND RESPECT. Children with low self-esteem are especially attracted to gangs because they perceive membership as a way of gaining recognition and respect from peers.

FOR EXCITEMENT. Those who are bored and lack a sense of direction may be fascinated by the gang lifestyle. Their infatuation may be reinforced by music and videos that glamorize gangs.

FOR PROTECTION. Those who feel threatened by gangs may join a rival gang to secure protection and a sense of power.

TO GAIN MATERIAL BENEFITS. Youths who live in poverty are especially attracted by the prospect of making fast money and obtaining material possessions from gang enterprise, usually by selling drugs.

TO SERVE AS AN OUTLET FOR THEIR ANGER. Many youths who join gangs have deep-seated feelings of anger, which may stem from a feeling of hopelessness about obtaining financial or material success and a strong sense of social injustice. They may see gang activities as opportunities to vent their rage.

TO JOIN IN WITH THEIR PEERS. Becoming a gang member may be perceived as the "cool" thing to do, and they may feel pressure to join to avoid being left out.

TO CONTINUE A FAMILY TRADITION. Parents who were previously gang members may subtly or directly encourage their child to join a gang. They may feel that a gang will provide their child with a sense of connectedness as well as a support system, but may not comprehend the genuine risks that gang membership poses.

Risk Factors for Joining a Gang

Youths with supportive family relationships and a strong sense of purpose are far less likely to be lured into a gang lifestyle than those who come from troubled homes where little guidance and few opportunities are afforded them. While no one risk factor leads to gang membership, the more factors an individual is exposed to, the more he is at risk of succumbing to the lure of a gang. The following factors cause youths to be especially vulnerable:

○ High level of gang activity in the community

○ Impoverished living conditions

○ Frequent moves from one community to another

○ History of family gang involvement

○ Family disorganization or discord

○ Victim of physical or emotional abuse

○ Lack of parental direction, involvement, and supervision

○ Large amount of unsupervised free time

○ Lack of involvement in community activities

○ Frequent exposure to music and movies glorifying gangs and violence

○ Involvement with delinquent peers

○ Drug and alcohol use

○ History of aggressive behavior

○ Feelings of low self-esteem and hopelessness

○ School attendance problems

○ Severe academic deficiencies

○ Limited employment opportunities

Signs of Gang Membership

It is not always easy for parents to know that their child has joined a gang because he may keep his affiliation secret. If you have concerns that your child is involved with a gang, monitor his behavior closely. The warning signs listed below may signal that he has joined or is considering joining a gang. Of course, no one characteristic necessarily signifies membership in a gang. Rather, look for a pattern of behavior that suggests gang affiliation.

- Wears clothing of the same color combination every day and has friends who wear the same type and color of clothing.

- Wears an extreme amount of jewelry with distinctive designs and only on one side of the body.

- Has tattoos with the name or initials of a gang, often displayed in Gothic script.

- Draws gang symbols, names, or initials on books, notebooks, on the walls or door of his room.

- Writes gang names, phrases, numbers, or initials under the brim of his hat.

- Is obsessed with music and videos that celebrate the gang lifestyle.

- Uses gang slang, which may include single letters, numbers, abbreviations, and terms understood only by other youths.

- Spends most of his time with members of a gang, who may be identified by their clothing of the same color, their tattoos with the name or initials of a gang, their listening to music with gang themes, and their greeting each other with hand signs.

- Stays out late and is secretive about where he has been and with whom.

- Uses hand signs with friends and practices them at home.

- Has pictures of himself and others displaying hand signs.
- Refuses to participate in family activities.
- Has undergone a marked change in attitude or behavior in school or at home.
- Is unusually defiant toward authority figures, including parents, teachers, and law enforcement officials.
- Has experienced a sudden decline in academic performance.
- Frequently cuts classes or skips school.
- Has large sums of money or expensive possessions that you cannot account for.
- Uses alcohol or drugs.
- Carries a weapon, such as a knife, gun, or box cutter.

Warning Signs That Your Child Is Doing Graffiti

To advertise their presence and mark their territory, gangs often use graffiti. Sometimes called the "newspaper of the streets," graffiti may include the gang's name, its symbols, and the nicknames of members, and it may be scrawled on public or private property. Gangs may also use graffiti to issue challenges or warnings to rival gangs and to communicate hateful messages. The presence of graffiti can create fear in a community, invite a violent response from a rival gang, and hasten the decline of a neighborhood; therefore, it is important for residents of a community to remove graffiti as soon as possible. In some communities property owners are required by law to remove graffiti promptly. Keep in mind that not all graffiti are the work of gangs. Gang graffiti are distinct from tagger graffiti, which are street drawings without gang content. If you think that your child may be involved in the spread of graffiti, look for the following warning signs:

- Has graffiti markings on his personal belongings.

- Reads graffiti magazines.

- Often comes home late at night.

- Frequently wears a backpack or baggy pants with large cargo-type pockets, which can be used for holding paint or other graffiti materials.

- Has graffiti materials in his possession, including spray paint, regular paint, markers, and etching tools.

- Has paint on his hands or clothing.

The Price of Membership

Gangs have the potential for drastically shaping the future of their members, usually in negative ways. And as the following list indicates, membership has its price—and it's a high one that can include any or all of the following:

- Requirement to commit violent or criminal acts as a condition of gang membership

- Minimal involvement with individuals outside of the gang, including family members

- Limited formal education

- Restricted opportunities for meaningful employment

- Belief that violence is a legitimate way to respond to problems

- Involvement in criminal or violent activities

- Criminal record

- Physical injury

- Alcohol and/or drug use

- Threats to family members

What You Can Do to Help Your Child Stay Out of Gangs

If you fear that your child may be at risk of becoming part of a gang in your community, take action before he becomes immersed in that lifestyle. You may have more power over your child than you think. Your role is particularly necessary if he does not appreciate the risks of being in a gang. The following strategies are especially important to pursue if you live in an area with a high level of gang activity.

- Talk with your child as early as elementary school about the risks of being in a gang. Make it clear to him that you disapprove of gangs and that they can result in physical injury or a criminal record.

- Learn about the gangs in your community, including their style of clothing, their symbols, their particular slang, their activities, and their hangouts.

- Talk with your child about what to do if he is pressured to join a gang. Role-play some situations and suggest some responses he can use to counter these pressures.

- Meet with your child's school counselor and ask for help in discouraging your child's gang involvement. Request that your child be placed in classes that do not have gang members in them.

- Discourage your child from wearing gang-style clothing. Wearing this clothing may not only signal to gang members his interest in joining but may also target him for violence from rival gangs.

- Get to know your child's friends and what activities he is doing with them. Find out their addresses and telephone numbers.

- Know the three "Ws": where your child is, who he is with, and what he is doing. Work out an arrangement for him to keep you posted if his plans change.

☼ Establish an evening curfew as well as a time when he must be home for dinner.

☼ Set some limits on the music your child listens to or the movies he watches. Consider not allowing him to watch very violent movies or to listen to music that glamorizes gangs or violence.

☼ Arrange for your child to be involved in activities after school or on weekends, such as scouts, recreational programs, art and music programs, tutoring, Boys & Girls Clubs, and Big Brothers/Big Sisters programs. If community activities are not available, look to your extended family for help in supervising your child.

☼ Arrange family activities that you know your child enjoys. Allow him to help choose these activities.

☼ If you live in an area with a high level of gang activity, establish some rules for your child such as the following:

  – He cannot associate with gang members or attend parties given by gangs.

  – He cannot hang out in areas where gangs congregate.

  – He cannot engage in any graffiti painting.

  – He cannot use hand signs in your presence.

  – He cannot write gang names or symbols or other gang graffiti on his personal belongings.

What if Your Child Is Already a Gang Member?

While your influence with your child will likely diminish if he joins a gang, you may still retain some leverage with him—and you certainly have the right to control what goes on in your household.

- Talk with your child about the risks of being in a gang, including physical injury and going to jail. Discuss these issues calmly. Yelling at him or berating him may only alienate him further and intensify his allegiance to the gang.

- If your police department has an antigang unit, talk with a member of this unit to gain information about your child's gang and how you can help get him out of it.

- Obtain help for your child from a school counselor, a community agency, a member of the antigang unit of the police department, or a member of the clergy.

- Do not allow gang members to congregate in your home.

- Inform your child that his friends are not welcome in your home if they are wearing gang clothing or carrying drugs or weapons.

- Notify the police if any gang member threatens you.

- Ask your child if he wants to leave the gang, and if so, help him take steps to do this. (See the next section.)

Rescuing Your Child from the Gang Lifestyle

Getting your child to commit to leaving a gang is an important but not easily achieved first step. Actually leaving the gang can be an even bigger challenge. The following is advice you can give your child as he attempts to separate from a gang:

- Find a family member or an adult in the community you trust to help you plan your strategy for leaving the gang. This might even be a member of the antigang unit of the police department.

- Do not tell gang members you want to leave the gang because it may give rise to physical retribution.

- Become more involved in school and community activities and less involved with gang members.

- Find a weekend or after-school job in the community.

- Avoid areas where gang members are known to congregate.

- Remove gang symbols from your personal belongings.

- Avoid wearing clothes and jewelry typical of the gang.

- Stop using gang language and signs.

- Do not take phone calls from gang members. Plan with family members some excuses they can use when gang members call.

- Talk with your guidance counselor and arrange to be moved to classes without gang members.

- If your school district permits, consider requesting a transfer to another school.

How You Can Help Combat Gangs in Your Community

Gangs can have a devastating impact on communities. They may terrorize residents by creating fear that they will be victims of a gang's illegal activities and violent acts. Members of a community who are organized and united in their determination to stem gang influence can play a vital role in making their neighborhood safer and more secure. The following are strategies that community members may pursue toward this end:

- Be willing to admit there is a gang problem in your community.

- Learn to recognize the signs of gang activity.

- Notify the police of any evidence of gang activity.

- Organize a citizen action group such as a Neighborhood Watch to monitor what is happening in your community and report suspicious activities or crimes in progress to the police.

- Offer organized activities for youths after school and on weekends through the schools, recreation departments, and youth organizations. These might include recreational, artistic, and musical activities, field trips, and tutoring.

- Work with local businesses to identify and create job opportunities for youth.

- Advocate for an antigang unit in your police department to track and monitor the activities of gangs.

- Report any evidence of graffiti to the police and organize your neighbors to remove it immediately after police examination. Find out if there is an agency or group that takes responsibility for removing graffiti. If not, you may want to organize a graffiti cleanup program.

- Start a graffiti hotline for residents to call to report graffiti in the community.

- Do not confront a person who is doing graffiti. This could result in injury to you. Instead, obtain a description of the individual and notify the police.

RECOMMENDED READING

Books for Kids

Dailey, D. C. (1999). *Use Your Brains, Stay Out of Gangs.* Littleton, CO: Brighter Horizons Publishing.

Loftis, C. (1996). *The Boy Who Sat by the Window: Helping Children Cope with Violence.* Far Hills, NJ: New Horizon Press (grades 3-6).

Randle, K. D. (1999). *Breaking Rank.* New York: Morrow Junior (for young adults).

Books for Parents

Christensen, L. W. (1999). *Gangbangers: Understanding the Deadly Minds of America's Street Gangs.* Boulder, CO: Paladin Press.

Sachs, S. L. (1997). *Street Gang Awareness: A Resource Guide for Parents and Professionals.* Minneapolis, MN: Fairview Press.

ORGANIZATIONS

Boys & Girls Clubs of America

1230 West Peachtree Street, NW
Atlanta, GA 30309
1-404-487-5700 (headquarters)
1-800-854-2582 (call to locate a club in your community)
www.bgca.org

> *Offers a program for disadvantaged youths in many communities to reduce gang involvement. Called Gang Prevention Through Targeted Outreach, it provides recreational and educational activities as well as counseling to at-risk youth.*

Gang Awareness Training Education (G.A.T.E.)

PMB #35
956 South Bartlett Road
Bartlett, IL 60103
home.flash.net/~bobomega/index.html

> *Uses local police officers to educate school-age youths about the dangers of gang involvement.*

Gang Resistance Education and Training (G.R.E.A.T.)

Bureau of Alcohol, Tobacco, and Firearms
650 Massachusetts Avenue
Washington, DC 20226
1-800-726-7070
www.atf.treas.gov/great/index.htm

> *Aims to reduce gang involvement and youth violence by providing structured activities and classroom instruction for middle school students by uniformed law enforcement officers.*

Mothers Against Gangs

1401 East Thomas Road
Phoenix, AZ 85014
1-602-235-9823
www.mothersagainstgangs.org

> *Encourages community efforts to divert youth from gang involvement and provides help to victims of gang violence.*

National Youth Gang Center

Institute for Intergovernmental Research
P. O. Box 12729
Tallahassee, FL 32317
1-850-385-0600
www.iir.com/nygc

A comprehensive source of information on gangs and program strategies.

Teens Against Gang Violence

2 Moody Street
Boston, MA 02124
1-617-282-9659
www.tagv.org

A volunteer, community-based, teen peer leadership program that provides violence, gun, and drug prevention programs for teens, parents, schools, and community groups.

CHAPTER 6

Keeping
Your Child Safe
from Gun Violence

Imagine that you are going about your morning routine. You have the television on and are listening to snatches of the morning show. Suddenly your local station breaks in for emergency coverage of a shooting spree. You hear the reporter's words but can hardly believe them: "We've just received word that a man burst into a classroom, pulled out a gun and started shooting at random, killing all twenty-four students in the class."

Now imagine that the scene is repeated two days later at another school. Twenty-four more students are shot and killed. This horrific news leaves you stunned and outraged.

You may think this is just morbid fiction and wonder why anyone would engage in such grim musings. But this is not an imaginary scenario. The reality is that every day on average twelve American children die from gun violence. The equivalent of a classroom of children is killed every other day by gunfire. But the public is hardly aware of this reality because this fact just doesn't have the urgency or the degree of sensationalism that the media thrives on. It's too routine to warrant attention.

Gun violence has reached the level of an epidemic in the United States. While many factors contribute to this problem, it is in large measure the result of the easy availability of firearms.

The federal government estimates that there are about 240 million guns in this country—nearly one for each man, woman, and child. This gives our country the dubious distinction of having one of the highest rates of gun ownership in the world.

While gun violence has had a staggering effect on American society, its impact has been especially pronounced among children and teens. A startling number have been killed by gunfire. Its impact also goes well beyond the actual victims. Children have lost family members and friends to gunfire, and are scared their lives will be cut short, are scared to walk to and from school or play outside for fear of being shot. And gun violence has had a devastating effect on the families that have lost children.

Federal law bans the possession of a handgun by a juvenile, but that isn't much of an impediment to the many youths who own or carry guns anyway. Fearful of peers with guns, they may obtain guns for protection, giving rise to a local arms race. And the shocking fact is that many young people have little difficulty obtaining firearms. Some need look no further than their own homes. A survey of children in the sixth through twelfth grades indicated that 59 percent believed they could obtain a gun; 35 percent said they could get a gun in less than an hour. Even if we consider that some of those surveyed were exaggerating or mistaken, these figures are alarming.

Confronting the problem of gun violence requires the combined efforts of legislators, gun manufacturers, law enforcement officials, school administrators, and parents. It also demands strong measures to control the sale, possession, and design of guns. Yet the United States has weaker gun control regulations than virtually any other industrialized nation. As just one example, there is no federal regulatory agency with the authority to require minimum design and safety standards on guns manufactured in this country. In short, guns are essentially exempt from consumer protection regulation.

While some contend that the Second Amendment of the Constitution automatically confers the right to own a gun and thus limits the ability of the government to regulate guns, judicial decisions say otherwise. According to a 1939 Supreme Court case *(United States v. Miller)*, owning a gun is only protected by the Constitution if it has "some reasonable relationship to the preservation or efficiency of a well-regulated militia." Indeed, no gun control measure has ever been overturned by a federal court based on the Second Amendment.

A recent study by the Harvard School of Public Policy indicated that most children want to live in a society with fewer guns, that they would feel safer if students did not bring guns to school, and that they would like society to keep youths from obtaining guns. This chapter takes a look at some of the steps we can take as parents and as a society to achieve these goals and to prevent senseless acts of gun violence against children, especially by keeping guns out of the hands of juveniles. As the following statistics indicate, the time has come for parents to take a stand and take action on keeping our children safe from gun violence.

Facts About Gun Violence in America

The following statistics paint a devastating picture of the toll that gun violence has exacted on American society.

- From 1979 to 1997 almost eighty thousand American youths were killed by gunfire, almost twenty-five thousand more than the number of American soldiers killed in the Vietnam War.

- In 1997, 4,205 children and teens were killed by firearms. This is equivalent to 90 school buses filled with children.

- Each day on average twelve American children ages one to nineteen are killed by gunfire. Put another way, a classroom of children is killed every other day by gunfire.

- A 1997 study indicated that American children under the age of fifteen are nearly twelve times more likely to die from gun violence than children in twenty-five industrialized nations combined.

- American teens are more likely to die from gunfire than from all the natural causes of death combined.

- The gun is the most commonly used method of committing suicide.

- Suicides are nearly five times more likely in households with a gun than those without a gun.

- In 1997, 306 juveniles under the age of twenty died as a result of accidental shootings.

- Guns can be found in 32 percent of households with children, according to a 1996 survey.

- Approximately 1.2 million latchkey children come home after school to a home with a gun and no adult supervision.

- One of every seventeen male high school students had carried a gun in the month preceding a 1998 survey.

- A 1993 survey indicated that one of every three children ages six to twelve feared his life would be cut short by gunfire.

- Injuries from gunfire are estimated to cost $40 billion a year in health care, public service, and lost work, with the vast majority of health care expenses paid for by the taxpayer.

Why Do Youths Carry Guns?

Guns have an unusual lure for many children and teens, especially males. Their curiosity may have been aroused by seeing guns used and sometimes glamorized on television, and in movies and video games. They may see guns and the people who use them as exciting. They may perceive guns as a source of power and protection. And some have come to believe that they must use guns to settle disputes. A 1998 study by the National Institute of Justice revealed the following reasons that a juvenile might carry a gun:

⊙ To protect himself

⊙ To gain respect and a sense of importance from others

⊙ To use in a crime

⊙ To gain revenge against someone

⊙ To hold it for a friend

⊙ To intimidate somebody

⊙ To conform with the behavior of friends

Safeguarding Your Child Against the Lure of Guns

As a parent you play a key role in helping your child learn to solve problems in a nonviolent manner and in keeping him from viewing guns as glamorous, exciting, or sources of power. Your role should include:

⊙ Modeling for your child how to resolve conflicts with others in a nonconfrontational, nonviolent manner

⊙ Talking with your child about how to avoid fights with peers and how to settle disputes without resorting to violence, and explaining that everybody becomes angry, but feelings can be expressed without hurting someone or using a weapon

⊙ Keeping guns out of your home

⊙ Not showing your child any gun you own for protection

⊙ Not glamorizing guns in any way

⊙ Discouraging gunplay by not buying your child toy guns

⊙ Participating in a toy gun buyback program if your child does have a toy gun; in this program toy guns are exchanged for other toys or for gift certificates.

⊙ Monitoring the programs your child watches to lessen his exposure to gun violence on television and in movies, mon-

itoring the video games he plays, and paying attention to the
Internet sites he visits

- Talking with your child about the gun violence he sees on
television, letting him know that guns hurt people in real
life; he may not understand this, especially if he see the victims of gunshots appearing on other shows.

- Teaching your child about the dangers of guns and the harm
they can cause even if you do not have a gun in your home,
because he may be exposed to guns outside of your home (at
a friend's home, for example)

- Informing your child that he is not to touch or play with
guns, whether in your home or in the home of a friend; tell
your child that if his friend brings out a gun, he should not
touch the gun, should leave the area immediately, and
should inform an adult about what happened.

- Not allowing your child to play at the home of a friend if it
contains an unlocked gun

- Contacting the Center to Prevent Handgun Violence to
find out how you and your child can view the video *Under
the Gun*, which helps viewers appreciate the dangers that
guns pose and the injury and anguish they can cause

- Making your voice heard by pressing local, state, and federal officials to adopt commonsense gun control regulations
such as those suggested later in this chapter

What if Your Child Has a Gun?

If you find that your child has a handgun, take immediate steps to
remove it from his possession and then learn his reasons for having
it. Impress on him the risks of gun ownership and do the following:

- Make it absolutely clear to your child that owning a handgun is unacceptable and insist that he turn it over to you
immediately.

- Try to understand why he feels it necessary to own a gun and then try to address these issues. If he tells you he needs to bring a gun to school for protection, talk with school officials about students who may be threatening or intimidating him. If necessary, consider a change of classes or even schools.

- Help your child understand that by carrying a gun he runs the risk of being reported to the police as well as becoming involved in a conflict with another person with a gun.

- Obtain counseling for your child so he can learn to manage his anger and settle disputes nonviolently.

- Find out if your community has a gun buyback program in which guns are exchanged for material incentives.

- Contact community agencies to find an educational program for juveniles with guns to help them understand the consequences of gun possession and violence.

- Ask your police department if it has a videotape you can watch with your child about the consequences of gun violence.

- Visit a support group of parents of gunshot victims with your child so he can experience the family consequences of gunfire.

- Call a nearby hospital with a trauma center to see if it has a program for juveniles to observe doctors treating victims of gunshot wounds. Talk with your child afterward about the impact of gun violence on victims and their families.

Precautions to Take if You Keep a Gun in Your Home

Carlos was like most six-year-olds. He loved to play games, especially one called "Pow Pow," in which he aimed a fake gun at himself and pretended to dodge the bullets. On Carlos's sixth birthday, as his godmother was decorating for his party, he found a real gun in her purse. He took it out and began playing "Pow Pow." Only this time the gun wasn't fake, and he couldn't dodge the bullets. He died on his birthday, shot in the neck by a .38 caliber bullet.

Carlos is one of many children who have died from accidental shootings. In 1997, 306 youths died this way. Many of these deaths could have been prevented if parents had taken some commonsense precautions in the home. Some are easy to implement, but unfortunately many gun owners are relatively lax in taking steps to prevent accidental shootings. About half of all gun owners do not keep their guns in a locked area, and about a quarter of them keep their guns unlocked and loaded. If you keep a gun in your home and are intent on providing the maximum protection to your family, consider the following safeguards. Most important, make sure the gun is unloaded and inaccessible to your child.

- Remove all firearms from your home, especially if you have children. While you may want a gun for protection, keep in mind that a gun kept in the home for protection is twenty-two times more likely to result in the death of a family member or friend than an intruder.

- As an alternative to owning a gun for protection, consider installing an alarm in your home, upgrading your door and window locks, or getting a dog.

- Do not rely on simply telling your child not to touch the gun. Curiosity may lead him to play with it despite your admonitions.

- Make sure the gun is unloaded.

- Keep the gun in a locked box or cabinet and put the keys in a place inaccessible to your child.

- Keep any ammunition stored and locked separately from the gun.

○ Make certain the gun has a safety-locking device such as a trigger lock. This is an inexpensive feature that, when properly used, can significantly reduce accidental shootings by children. (Some communities have given trigger locks to gun owners for free.)

○ Make sure the gun has a load indicator to show whether it is loaded.

○ If you own guns to use for target practice, consider keeping them at the shooting range.

○ Find out if your community offers a course or program on gun safety.

○ Call the state or local police to find out what state law requires you to do if you have a gun in your home.

○ Ask the sponsoring organizations or your pediatrician to arrange for you to participate in an educational program for parents entitled Steps to Prevent Firearm Injury, which is offered jointly by the American Academy of Pediatrics and the Center to Prevent Handgun Violence. (See *Organizations* on page 122).

How Your Child Can Help End Gun Violence

The following are some proactive steps that you can encourage your child to take to decrease gun possession and use among his peers:

○ Become educated about gun violence by attending community programs to discuss the risks of gun ownership.

○ Inform school administrators of students whom he suspects of carrying guns (insist his name be kept anonymous) or call a "weapons hotline."

○ Sign the Student Pledge Against Gun Violence (see *Organizations* on page 122) in which students promise never to bring a gun to school or settle conflicts with a gun, and to keep friends from using a gun to settle a conflict.

⊙ If your child is a high school student, ask permission from the school administration to give talks to elementary and middle school students about the risks of gun use.

⊙ Participate in the Hands Without Guns campaign to reduce the demand for guns by youths. This is sponsored by the Educational Fund to End Handgun Violence.

⊙ Help organize a march against gun violence.

⊙ Organize or participate in a toy gun buyback program in which toy guns are exchanged for gift certificates or other toys that appeal to children.

What Society Can Do to Lessen Gun Violence

The United States has weaker gun regulations than any other industrialized country. England and Japan, for example, have banned private ownership of virtually all handguns. The absence of effective gun control measures in the United States helps explain why the rates of gun deaths from homicide, suicide, and accidental shootings are far greater here than in most other industrialized nations. Surveys indicate that the public supports a wide range of measures to regulate firearms, but the gun lobby seems to have a louder voice than the public. To counteract the National Rifle Association and its powerful lobby, contact your elected officials and let them know that you support the following measures (see Gun Free Kids under *Organizations* on page 122 for information on how to contact your federal, state, and local officials):

- Give a federal agency the authority to regulate the design and manufacture of guns and ammunition.

- Require that all handguns be registered with the government.

- Require that all handgun owners be licensed and trained in the use of the weapon.

- Ban the sale of all assault weapons.

- Require a police permit before a gun can be purchased.

- Ban the sale of guns through the mail or over the Internet.

- Require background checks on people buying guns at gun shows.

- Tighten the restrictions on gun dealers.

- Set strict limits on the number of guns an individual can purchase.

- Prohibit individuals from carrying a concealed weapon unless they are specifically authorized.

- Prohibit individuals who have been convicted of a violent misdemeanor from owning guns.

- Regulate the sale of ammunition for handguns.

- Make gun owners criminally responsible when they permit a child access to a firearm that causes injury.

- Make gun manufacturers liable for injuries resulting from defective guns.

- Require that serial numbers on firearms be tamper resistant.

- Require gun manufacturers to design new guns with safety features, including child-safety locks.

- Develop "smart-gun" technology that limits the use of a gun to an authorized person.

RECOMMENDED READING

Books for Kids

Cox, V. (1997). *Guns, Violence, and Teens.* Springfield, NJ: Enslow Publishers (for young adults).

Dailey, D. C. (1999). *Guns Are Not for Fun.* Littleton, CO: Brighter Horizons Publishing.

Miller, M. (1999). *Coping with Weapons and Violence in School and on Your Streets.* New York: Rosen Publishing Group (for young adults).

Schulson, R. E. (1997). *Guns: What You Should Know.* Morton Grove, IL: Albert Whitman & Company (ages 4-8).

Books for Parents

Murray, J. M. (1994). *50 Simple Things You Can Do About Guns: A Citizen's Guide to Saving Lives and Stopping Gun Violence.* San Francisco: Robert D. Reed. (To obtain a copy, send $9.95 to Robert D. Reed Publishing Company, 750 La Playa, Suite 647, San Francisco, CA 94121, or call 1-800-774-7336.)

National Rifle Association. (1995). *A Parent's Guide to Gun Safety.* Fairfax, VA: National Rifle Association.

ORGANIZATIONS

Center to Prevent Handgun Violence

1225 Eye Street, NW, Suite 1100
Washington, DC 20005
1-202-898-0792
www.handguncontrol.org

Plays a significant role in advocating for gun control legislation.

Coalition to Stop Gun Violence

1023 15th Street, NW, Suite 600
Washington, DC 20005
1-202-408-0061
www.csgv.org

Dedicated to stopping gun violence by fostering community and national action.

Fight Crime: Invest in Kids

2000 P Street, NW, Suite 240
Washington, DC 20036
1-202-776-0027
www.fightcrime.org

An advocacy and crime-prevention organization made up of sheriffs, police chiefs, prosecutors, victims of violence, and leaders of police officer organizations.

Gun Free Kids

332 Bleecker Street
Box E-9
New York, NY 10014
1-212-674-3710
www.gunfreekids.org

This Internet action center makes it easy for citizens to ask their national and local elected officials to support legislation that will help keep guns away from children. Visitors to the site can access a list of elected officials and can contact them through links. The site also provides up-to-date information on gun control issues.

Project Home Safe

11 Mile Hill Road
Newtown, CT 06470
1-203-426-1320
www.projecthomesafe.org

A nationwide program to encourage safe firearms handling and secure storage practices through safety education and the distribution of free gun-locking devices.

Student Pledge Against Gun Violence

112 Nevada Street
Northfield, MN 55057
1-507-645-5378
www.pledge.org

The pledge commits young people to take an active role in reducing gun violence.

Women Against Gun Violence

P. O. Box 1501
Culver City, CA 90232-1501
1-310-204-2348
www.wagv.org

Works to end tolerance of gun violence by educating the public about its costs and dangers.

CHAPTER 7

Helping Your Child Say "No" to Drugs, Alcohol, and Tobacco

Kevin had always been a good kid, and his parents often said to each other how lucky they were to have a kid like him. He was a good student, excelling in several subjects; he was a good athlete and especially enjoyed being on a Little League team; he was likable and had many friends; and he had a good sense of humor and was a pleasure to be around. But lately his parents noticed a change in his behavior and even in his personality. It all started a few months into his freshman year of high school. His grades started dropping— more than a change of routine could account for—and he was frequently sullen and kept to himself; often he stayed in his room, wanting as little communication with his parents as possible. Another change that alarmed Kevin's parents was that he no longer kept in touch with his old circle of friends. His social contacts were limited to two boys who seemed to have the same aloof attitudes as Kevin.

Kevin's parents were at a loss. They couldn't understand what brought such a change over their son, until one day when Kevin's mother was checking his jeans pockets before putting them in the wash. She found a plastic sandwich bag containing a small amount of what looked like marijuana. After overcoming her initial feelings of shock and denial, she realized that she now had an explanation for the sudden changes in Kevin's demeanor. What she didn't know was what she should do next.

A child's getting involved with drugs or alcohol is the biggest fear many parents face as their children reach the teen years. A child with drug or alcohol problems can leave parents drained of energy, filled with fear, and wondering what went wrong. In the struggle to help their child resolve a problem that he may deny is a problem, parents may find themselves riding an emotional roller coaster of anger, anxiety, depression, embarrassment, frustration, and guilt.

Unfortunately, many parents of today's teens have ridden this roller coaster. Drug and alcohol use is a pervasive problem among adolescents; indeed, substance use may be the biggest challenge teenagers face. Abuse of drugs or alcohol can drastically alter a teenager's life and has the potential of leading to a range of difficult consequences, from physical and emotional problems to school failure, legal problems, injury, or even death. The long-term threat from another seemingly less dangerous substance, tobacco, is on a par with those from drugs and alcohol. The fact is that more than 5 million youths living today will die prematurely due to a smoking-related disease.

In trying to discourage your own child from substance use, you may underestimate your influence. You may assume that the opinions of your child's peers count more than your own. While it is true that peers have considerable impact on a teen's beliefs and behavior, the reality is that you also play an important role in shaping your child's attitudes. Research indicates that when it comes to major issues in teens' lives, parents command the most influence. As just one example, teens who have parents who talk with them about the risks of drug use are much less likely to use drugs.

In spite of this encouraging data, parents still face formidable obstacles in discouraging a child's drug or alcohol use. A prominent concern is teens' easy access to drugs, alcohol, and tobacco. A second challenge is the media. Advertising tends to glorify alcohol use and ignore its harmful effects. Although you may feel that advertisements for alcohol are targeted at an audience older than your teen, the advertising gimmicks and slogans often become part of youth culture. For example, one recent ad campaign featured a group of twenty-something guys yelling the now ubiquitous question "Whassup?" into the phone. Before long this phrase became a favorite line of schoolchildren as young as six. Though the association between that expression and an alcoholic beverage may not be apparent to a very young child, advertising that young viewers find appealing is certain to leave a lasting impression as to the "coolness" of the product being advertised. As for tobacco use, a recent study indicated that advertising plays an even greater role than peer pressure in influencing teens to smoke. Another hurdle that parents may face is their child's lack of concern for the consequences of substance abuse. Many teens have a false sense of invulnerability, feeling that they are somehow immune to the negative effects of drugs, alcohol, and tobacco.

Parents may not always take full advantage of their leverage with their child. Denial and lack of information are often the culprits. Parents frequently perceive drugs and alcohol as a serious societal problem but are blind to the possibility (or even the reality) of their own child's involvement. They may not know the signs of substance use. Even if they have their suspicions, they may not know what to say or do. And if they do confront their child with their suspicions, they may be deceived by his response that he is not using or that it was only a one-time thing.

When it comes to drugs, alcohol, or tobacco, the stakes are too high for you to ignore the possibility that your child is at risk. Accept what the experts say—that you have considerable impact on your child's decisions with regard to substance use—and take an active role in trying to influence his beliefs and behaviors. And don't wait until your child enters high school to begin shaping his views. The reality is that by then many kids have already tried their first cigarette, had their first drink, or experimented with drugs.

In this chapter you will find the information, insights, and guidance needed to help your child rise above the adolescent pressure to be "cool" by participating in risky behaviors. You will also find information on how to get him the help he needs if he is already engaging in this harmful behavior.

Facts About Teen Drug and Alcohol Use

- Teenagers identify drugs as the single most important problem they face.

- Obtaining drugs and alcohol is very easy, according to teenagers. In a survey of high school students, almost half reported that they could buy marijuana within one hour.

- The younger a person is when he begins to use alcohol or drugs, the more likely he is to develop drug- or alcohol-related problems.

- In a national survey of sixth graders, half reported that they felt peer pressure to drink alcohol.

- The transition from age twelve to thirteen signals a dramatic increase in children's exposure to drugs.

- A recent study indicated that 28 million people age twelve and older used illicit drugs in the previous year.

- The initial use of alcohol often occurs during the early teen years. Sixty percent of teens who have used alcohol report that they had their first drink by ninth grade.

- Four out of every five twelfth graders have used alcohol at least once, based on a recent survey. Among those who had used alcohol within the past month, more than half had engaged in binge drinking (consuming five or more drinks in a row).

- Thirty-five percent of seventeen-year-olds reported that pot was available at most parties they attended in the previous six months, while 54 percent said that alcohol was available at most parties.

- Teens who use drugs or alcohol are more likely to have low self-esteem, which results in lack of confidence or security to resist negative peer pressure.

- Teens who have used marijuana are nine times likelier to get drunk at least once a month.

- Teens who have drunk alcohol are four times likelier to smoke marijuana.

- Young people who use alcohol or drugs are more likely to be involved in violent incidents, have unprotected sex, have academic problems, and be injured in a car accident due to driving while impaired.

- Twenty-three percent of teenagers report that they have driven after drinking.

- The number one cause of death among Americans fifteen to twenty-four years of age is alcohol-related automobile accidents.

- Drugs and alcohol have been linked to a range of serious or fatal injuries, including spinal cord injuries, drowning, bicycle accidents, and fires.

Some Common Drugs Used by Teens

Some drugs that teens are exposed to are given below, along with their warning signs:

MARIJUANA. This is the most widely used illegal drug in America and is often the first drug used by teens. The marijuana available today is generally more potent than it was in the 1960s. Commonly referred to as pot, weed, grass, or dope, marijuana is usually smoked and stays in the brain for as long as thirty days. Marijuana users may exhibit red, bloodshot eyes, dilated pupils, a dry mouth, sleepiness, unusual hunger, poor coordination, slow thinking, impaired memory and judgment, and lessened motivation. It may also impede their ability to drive. Frequent use can lead to anxiety and depression. Marijuana can pose serious health risks if used with alcohol.

LSD (LYSERGIC ACID DIETHYLAMIDE). This hallucinogenic drug is taken orally and can give rise to hallucinations (imagined experiences that appear real) and sensory distortions, which may frighten the user. Often called acid, LSD may also cause a person to have mood swings and feel suspicious and out of control. Users may have a hard time communicating or concentrating and may experience sleeplessness, trembling, and increased heart rate and blood pressure. The effects of hallucinogens can last up to twelve hours.

PCP (PHENCYCLIDINE). Often referred to as angel dust, this hallucinogenic drug can be taken orally or injected or smoked. It can cause irrational fears, anxiety, a feeling of detachment, and extreme disorientation. Users may lose coordination and are thus prone to accident and injury. Other hallucinogenic drugs include mescaline and peyote.

COCAINE. This is a stimulant that can provide temporary pleasure and a feeling of unlimited energy, but it is often followed by depression and a craving for more of the drug. A person who uses "coke" may become restless, irritable, fearful, and even paranoid. Typically inhaled through the nose, cocaine can affect one's blood pressure, breathing, and heart rate. "Crack" is a form of cocaine that has been chemically altered and can be smoked. Both cocaine and crack are highly addictive, can dominate a person's life, and can cause the user to engage in risky behavior.

AMPHETAMINE. Often called speed or an upper, this stimulant can cause anxiety, restlessness, and changes in blood pressure and heart rate. Methamphetamine is a very strong and potentially dangerous form of amphetamine that comes in crystals (called ice) or powder (called crank). Ritalin, a stimulant medication used by children with attention deficit disorder, is sometimes used by teens for its energizing effects.

ECSTASY. This amphetamine-like substance is widely used by teens. A stimulant to the central nervous system, it can also have hallucinogenic effects. It leaves the user feeling peaceful and energized, but after the high he may feel tired and depressed. Ecstasy is popular at clubs because it allows the user to dance and stay alert for hours without getting tired.

BARBITURATE. Often called a downer, this drug has the opposite effect of amphetamines by slowing down the nervous system. When taken in small doses it can help a person relax. It can result in physical injury due to impairment of coordination, reflexes, and judgment. Users may display slurred speech, drowsiness, dilated pupils, and tremors.

INHALANT. Teens may inhale vapors from common products such as glue, household cleaners, hairspray, spray paint, and gasoline to produce mind-altering effects. It can cause confusion, mood swings, slowed reactions, impaired judgment, headaches, dizziness, and nausea. In some cases it can lead to serious physical injury. About one in five teenagers reports having used an inhalant, with use heaviest in eighth grade.

DRUG OR ALCOHOL USE MAY CAUSE . . .

. . . *physical problems.* Both drugs and alcohol can lead to health problems even before the user reaches the stage of chronic use or addiction. Drugs can cause a variety of physical effects, depending on the particular drug, including increased heart rate and blood pressure, chest pain, dizziness, headache, nausea, blurred vision, fever, muscle spasms, and seizures. In extreme cases they can precipitate a heart attack, stroke, or respiratory failure. Chronic alcohol use can lead to serious health problems, including high blood pressure, heart attack, stroke, colitis, ulcers, kidney and liver problems, and various forms of cancer. Both alcohol and drug use can cause lack of physical coordination, which may result in injuries from falls.

. . . *psychological problems.* Depending on the drug, these may include hallucinations, sensory distortions, anxiety, depression, paranoia, violent or erratic behavior, impaired judgment, and confusion. Frequent alcohol use may lead to many of these same problems and may also lessen inhibitions so that an individual may be more prone to fighting.

. . . *problems of addiction.* Users of alcohol and some drugs can develop an addiction so that they must continue to use the substance to function normally. They may also develop a tolerance to certain drugs so that they need more of the drug to achieve the same effects.

. . . *interpersonal problems.* Drug and alcohol use can cause a teen to withdraw from his friends and family, creating an uncomfortable psychological barrier. In addition, he may find that his friends are no longer interested in being with him because of his substance abuse.

. . . *academic problems.* A teen abusing alcohol or drugs may have difficulty concentrating in school, remembering information, and completing schoolwork. Attendance and disciplinary problems may also surface.

. . . *motivational problems.* This may be evident not only in the child's lack of attention to schoolwork but also in his lack of caring for friends and family. In addition, he may have less commitment to previously expressed post–high school ambitions.

. . . *legal problems.* Being caught with drugs can result in a child's having a police record. Similarly, being under the influence of alcohol in a public setting or while driving may have legal consequences.

. . . *financial problems.* A teen using drugs or alcohol may find that he has little money left over after purchasing alcohol or drugs, or not enough money to buy the drugs he feels he needs. This may lead to frequent borrowing or even taking money from parents or stealing from others. Being under the influence of either drugs or alcohol will no doubt affect a person's work perform- ance and may lead to his firing. Some employers even require drug testing prior to hiring an individual.

. . . *increased risk while driving.* A teen under the influence of drugs or alcohol is at increased risk for having a car accident. The number of teenagers who are injured or lose their lives in alcohol-related car accidents is staggering. Car accidents are the number one killer of young people, with more than half involv- ing alcohol use.

. . . *unprotected sex.* Alcohol or drug use may lessen a person's in- hibition and impair his judgment, often resulting in poor deci- sion-making with regard to sex. This may lead to pregnancy as well as sexually transmitted diseases.

. . . *date rape.* Date rape often happens when a boy takes advantage of a girl who has been using alcohol or drugs. A boy who has been drinking may become sexually aggressive and may ignore or mis- interpret a girl's signals, or may take a "no" for a "yes."

. . . *disruption of family life.* The impact of drug or alcohol use ex- tends beyond the user and can be especially distressing and dis- ruptive to family members. It has been estimated that for every person who has a drug or alcohol problem, at least four others are affected by the behavior.

Why Teens Use Drugs and Alcohol

When asked why they use drugs or alcohol, the reasons given by teens are many and varied, and can include one or several of the following:

- ☉ To be accepted by and fit in with their peers
- ☉ To escape from upsetting problems
- ☉ To lessen uncomfortable feelings such as anger or loneliness
- ☉ To reduce stress and anxiety

- To decrease social inhibitions and increase social confidence
- To appear more grown up
- To feel good
- To satisfy their curiosity
- To seek thrills
- To rebel against their parents

How to Tell if Your Teen Is Using Drugs or Alcohol

Although being suspicious of your teen and showing a lack of trust in his judgment can be harmful to your relationship with him, being unaware of a teen's drug or alcohol use can be harmful to his health and well-being. The following behaviors may signal that your child is using drugs or alcohol, but bear in mind that they may also be caused by other problems. Whatever the cause, a pattern of these behaviors warrants your concern and follow-up.

- Hanging out with peers who use drugs or alcohol
- Loss of interest in activities that he previously enjoyed
- Significant decline in school performance or attendance
- Frequent conflicts with family members
- Physical changes, which may include red, bloodshot eyes, dilated pupils, frequent sore throat or runny nose, wheezing, bags under eyes, and bruises from falls
- Nausea and vomiting
- Fatigue or drowsiness
- Change in sleeping habits
- Change in eating habits or unexplained weight loss
- Poor coordination

- Slurred speech
- Low motivation and lack of energy
- Sudden lack of concern for appearance
- Confused thinking and impaired judgment
- Difficulty remembering
- Unusual secretiveness about actions and possessions
- Extreme mood swings
- Appearance of being withdrawn and isolated
- Depressed mood or suicidal thoughts
- Hostile, uncooperative attitude
- Possession of drug paraphernalia such as pipes, cigarette papers, or medicine bottles
- Clothing with drug-related messages
- Frequently being short of cash and borrowing or taking money
- Alcohol on breath
- Frequent use of eyedrops or breath mints
- Missing or watered-down alcohol in the home
- Odor of gas or household products
- Unexplained paint around mouth or on hands

YOUR CHILD IS LESS LIKELY TO USE DRUGS OR ALCOHOL IF HE . . .

. . . has friends who do not use alcohol or drugs.

. . . is involved in school or community activities.

. . . is involved with a church or synagogue.

. . . has positive feelings about school.

. . . is experiencing school success.

. . . has a strong bond with his parents.

. . . has parents who provide him with encouragement and emotional support.

. . . has parents who get involved in his activities.

. . . has respect for his parents' point of view.

. . . feels he can discuss social concerns with his parents.

. . . has parents who offer sound guidance in coping with peer issues.

. . . has parents who make their expectations clear and set reasonable limits.

. . . is expected to comply with his parents' expectations.

. . . experiences reasonable and nonpunitive consequences for violating his parents' rules.

. . . has parents who provide close supervision and monitoring of him.

. . . eats dinner with his family on a regular basis.

. . . has siblings who discourage substance use.

How You Can Discourage Your Child from Using Drugs or Alcohol

Your child's views about drugs and alcohol begin to take form at an early age, long before he is first offered a beer or a joint, so you need to start shaping his attitudes toward substance use during his elementary school years. The following are some steps you can take to discourage his use of drugs and alcohol:

NURTURE YOUR RELATIONSHIP WITH YOUR CHILD. You will have more leverage with your child with regard to drug and alcohol issues if you have a strong bond with him. You can strengthen this connection by spending time with him on a regular basis and doing activities you know he likes. Also make a point of eating meals together as a family as often as possible. (One study showed that teens whose families ate together five or more times per week were less likely to be involved with drugs or alcohol.) This is a good time to find out what is happening at school, what is happening with friends, and what concerns your child may have.

ACCENTUATE THE POSITIVE. Teens with low self-esteem are especially prone to drug or alcohol use. Try to boost your child's confidence and support his self-worth by giving him frequent praise. Focus more on what he does right and restrain your impulse to be critical.

CONVEY YOUR EXPECTATIONS CLEARLY. Make it crystal clear to your child that you do not want him using drugs or alcohol. Discuss with him the possible physical and psychological effects of substance use. The section in this chapter about the problems associated with drug and alcohol use provides a good starting point for this discussion.

TAKE ADVANTAGE OF TEACHABLE MOMENTS TO TALK WITH YOUR CHILD ABOUT DRUGS AND ALCOHOL. Your child may be more receptive to talking about these issues if the subject comes up naturally and he does not feel that the topic is being forced on him. This may be, for example, when the topic comes up on a television show or when you hear of a youngster in the community who is struggling with a substance abuse problem. In talking with your child, consider working in the following points:

- Discuss the possible effects of using drugs and alcohol.
- Let him know that possessing, buying, or selling drugs is against the law and that a drug-related arrest could have serious and long-term consequences for him.
- He may tell you that just about everybody does it. Let him know this is not the case, that millions of teens do not drink or use drugs and that his friends will likely accept his decision not to use them.
- Tell your child that using alcohol or drugs can lead to unplanned or unprotected sex, which can lead to sexually transmitted disease or pregnancy.

- Point out that advertising tends to glamorize drinking and does not mention the potentially harmful effects.

- In addition to talking about what drugs and alcohol will do, let him know what they will not do: they will not solve his problems, they will not help him learn, they will not make him more popular, they will not help him become more mature, and they will not help develop his mind or body.

ENCOURAGE YOUR CHILD TO BE OPEN WITH YOU. Your child will face some awkward and difficult situations during his teen years and will be better able to respond to them if he feels he has your ear. Getting your teen to feel comfortable talking with you can be a challenge. It requires, first and foremost, that you listen carefully and attentively to what he says and that you do not bombard him with advice. If you come across as having all the answers, he will likely be discouraged from talking with you in the future. Ask questions to clarify his concerns or his thinking, let him know when you agree with him, and compliment him when he has made a wise decision. If he makes statements about drugs or alcohol that challenge your views, respond in a calm manner while offering your own perspective.

BE A GOOD ROLE MODEL. As the saying goes, "Actions speak louder than words." When it comes to teaching your child to be responsible in his attitudes toward drugs and alcohol, examine your own patterns of substance use to make sure you are modeling responsible and safe behavior. If you abuse alcohol or drugs, your message to your teen to abstain may fall on deaf ears. Set a good example by not using drugs and using alcohol in moderation if at all. In considering the impact of your own drinking behavior on your child, ask yourself the following questions: Do you drink during every holiday and celebration? Are social gatherings in your home focused on drinking? Do you take a drink every time you face a stressful situation? If you answer yes to any of these questions, you may want to modify your drinking patterns.

DISCOURAGE YOUR CHILD'S INVOLVEMENT WITH ALCOHOL IN YOUR HOME. You might want to restrict his access to your supply of alcohol or your prescription drugs. Do not give him alcohol, except perhaps for a religious ceremony. Also, do not involve your child in your alcohol use by having him get you a beer or teaching him how to mix a drink.

SET REASONABLE LIMITS. While teens seek freedom and independence, many still desire structure, guidance, and, yes, even limits. Establish selective and reasonable limits related to possible drug or alcohol use without overwhelming your child with rules. For example, set a curfew and stick with it (with exceptions for special occasions). Impose reasonable but not harsh consequences for his violation of the rules.

MONITOR YOUR CHILD'S FRIENDS AND ACTIVITIES. Be aware of whom your child is spending time with, the activities he and his friends are involved in, and the places they are going. When his peer group is on the right track, you can have peace of mind that he is probably headed in the same direction. In addition to getting to know his friends, try to get to know his friends' parents.

HELP YOUR CHILD LEARN TO DEAL WITH PEER PRESSURE. He is likely to encounter pressure from peers to drink or do drugs during his teen years. You can help give him the tools to resist this pressure. Let him know you understand that dealing with these pressures can be tough. If he is receptive, try role-playing with him some ways of responding to peers. You might offer him statements he can use, such as the following:

- "No, thanks. I'm not into drinking."
- "I have other plans tonight. Melissa and I are going to the mall."
- "I need to stay in shape for the basketball season."
- "I don't want to gain any weight."
- "I can't stand the taste."
- "I can't. I'm driving tonight."

BE ACCESSIBLE TO YOUR CHILD AFTER SCHOOL. The after-school hours can be troublesome for teens and a time when some begin experimenting with drugs or alcohol. If your child is on his own after school because of your work demands, find a way to keep tabs on where he is and what he is doing. Make sure he knows your number at work and the number of your cell phone if you have one. Consider getting him a phone card to use for these occasions. You might arrange for him to check in with you at a regular time.

ENCOURAGE YOUR CHILD'S INVOLVEMENT IN ORGANIZED ACTIVITIES. If he is involved in school or community activities, there will be less time and opportunity for him to engage in unhealthy ventures. In addition, these activities are a good way for him to meet peers who are positive influences. While you want to avoid placing constant pressure on him to join activities if he is resistant, you may need to nudge him a bit. If he is a risk-taker and you fear he may seek drugs or alcohol to satisfy his sense of adventure and test his limits, you might try to find a daring but safe activity that he might try instead.

HELP YOUR CHILD COPE WITH STRESS. Some teens resort to drugs or alcohol to help relieve stress. If you think your child is stressed out, find ways to help him. Give him emotional support—a hug, a pat on the back, some encouraging words—before or after an anxiety-provoking situation. You might help him learn some relaxation techniques such as deep breathing or yoga, or you might offer him the option of seeing a counselor to discuss his concerns.

BE EMPHATIC ABOUT DRINKING AND DRIVING. Emphasize to your child that under no circumstances is he to drive while under the influence of alcohol or drugs. And if your smart-alecky child asks you whether that means it's okay to drink or do drugs as long as he's not driving, make it clear that that's prohibited as well. Of course, if you've clearly imparted that lesson, starting in the early and preteen years, he will already know this. Similarly, instruct him that he is not allowed to be in a car driven by someone who is under the influence. Make it clear that he can call you to pick him up at any time if he feels he would be putting himself at risk by riding with someone else. Make sure he understands that you would not be angry at receiving such a call but would be pleased at his show of good judgment.

TEACH YOUR CHILD HOW TO MAKE GOOD DECISIONS. Teens who use drugs or alcohol may be poor decision-makers. Help your child learn to make wise decisions by considering the following questions:

- What is the decision I'm faced with?
- What do I need to find out before making this decision?
- Where can I get reliable information?
- What are the positive and negative consequences of the decision?
- What is the best decision for me in light of these potential consequences?

EXPRESS CONFIDENCE IN YOUR CHILD'S ABILITY TO BE RESPONSIBLE. If you feel that he can be trusted to make wise decisions, tell him. By conveying your trust in him, he will likely be motivated not to want to betray that trust. The reverse is also the case: if you try to control every aspect of his behavior and show little faith in his ability to make the right decision, he may be more inclined to go against your wishes. If you treat him in a grown-up manner, he is more likely to act grown up. This does not mean, however, that you do not need to give him some cautions about drugs or alcohol or that you should let him off the hook if he is found to be using them.

ENCOURAGE YOUR CHILD TO AVOID PARTIES WITH DRUGS OR ALCOHOL. If you are confident that he has the strength and maturity to refuse the overtures of his peers to drink or use drugs, you may feel better about his attending these parties. Let him know, however, that if he is uncomfortable at a party because of the presence of drugs or alcohol, he can call you and you will pick him up immediately. If you are concerned about an upcoming party he is going to, consider calling the parents whose home is the site of the party and check that there will be adults present and that alcohol or drugs will not be available.

MAKE SURE YOUR CHILD'S PARTIES ARE FREE OF DRUGS AND ALCOHOL. Your child may try to persuade you to allow alcohol at his party. Hold your ground, letting him know that this is a non-negotiable issue. Also inform him that one or both parents will be at home during the party.

ADVOCATE FOR DRUG AND ALCOHOL EDUCATION IN SCHOOL. Many schools provide this instruction as part of the health curriculum. You may also want to support a school policy of "zero tolerance" of drugs and alcohol both during the school day and at school-sponsored activities.

What to Do if Your Child Is Abusing Drugs or Alcohol

Helping a child who is experiencing substance abuse may tax your resources to the limit. He may deny that he has a problem and resist getting professional help. Consider taking the following steps if you find that your child is using drugs or alcohol:

TRUST YOUR INSTINCTS. If you suspect your child is using drugs or alcohol, go with your gut. Don't drop the issue because he denies your suspicions. Denials are par for the course for substance abusers.

ASSESS THE URGENCY OF THE PROBLEM. In doing a preliminary assessment of whether your child is a problem drinker or drug user (as opposed to a one-time experimenter), consider the degree to which his substance use is affecting his:

- school performance
- work obligations

- relationships with family members
- relationships with peers
- physical health
- mental health

SPEAK IN A CALM, UNEMOTIONAL, BUT HONEST MANNER. Finding out that your child is using drugs or alcohol on a regular basis may be shocking and is obviously very upsetting. Take a day or two to sort out your feelings before you talk with him. When you do—and this discussion should not be put off very long—let him know that you take his drinking or using of drugs very seriously. Tell him why you feel it can be harmful to him, physically, psychologically, academically, and legally. Be prepared for his denial that he is using or, if he acknowledges his use, that it is hurting him in any way. Give him a chance to talk and be sure to listen attentively without lecturing or pleading. In a calm but forceful way let him know that his behavior cannot continue and that you need to take steps to help him. Tell him that you will support him as he gets help but that you will not accept his continued use.

DO NOT CONFRONT YOUR CHILD WHEN HE IS HIGH. Wait until he is free of the influence of drugs or alcohol and in a reasonable mood.

DO NOT PUNISH YOUR CHILD. While you may be angry with him for his substance use, punishing him is unlikely to be helpful. Of course, you may want to restrict his activities and set tighter limits to lessen the chance of his substance abuse, but punishing or threatening him may only embroil you in an angry exchange, intensify his desire to drink or use alcohol, and reduce the chance that he will cooperate with you. It may also distract you from your goal, which is to get him to stop and to get him some help.

AVOID EMOTIONAL RESPONSES. Do not make accusations, call him names, or be sarcastic. Emotional appeals may only serve to increase his feelings of guilt and intensify his desire to drink or do drugs.

Get Professional Help. You can obtain help from a variety of sources, such as:

- an alcohol or drug hotline (check the telephone directory under "drug abuse," "alcohol abuse," or "crisis services")
- a substance abuse counselor in your child's school
- a community mental health agency
- a private counselor (preferably someone certified in assessing and treating substance abuse)
- Alcoholics Anonymous
- an in-patient drug or alcohol treatment program

Keep in mind that treatment for substance abuse can take time and may involve setbacks and relapses. With professional help and your support, your child is likely to improve.

Stay the Course. Your child may insist he does not have a problem and resist your efforts to get him help. Do not accept his pleas that he will stop. Even if he were to stop, which is unlikely, his substance use may reflect underlying problems that require attention. This painful experience requires courage and strength on your part, and you need to hold your ground and obtain help for your child.

Do Not Protect Your Child from the Consequences of His Drug or Alcohol Use. Your instinct may be to make excuses for his behavior, cover up for his actions, blame yourself, or shield him from the consequences of his behavior, but you won't be doing him any favors if you choose this approach. In order to be motivated to change, he needs to experience the consequences of his behavior.

Help Your Child Receive Support from Other Adults. It is not uncommon for teens to find it easier to talk with an adult other than their parents about sensitive or difficult subjects. If your child is not receptive to talking with you, try to find someone he trusts who will serve as an objective sounding board, such as a grandparent, uncle, family friend, sibling, guidance counselor, teacher, or coach. This person may be effective in helping your child stop his drinking or drug use. Children often do not want to disappoint an important adult figure in their lives.

GET HELP FOR YOURSELF. Dealing with a substance-abusing child may be the hardest and most painful thing you will ever have to do as a parent. It may drain every ounce of your energy and send you on an emotional roller-coaster ride. You may find that you need to talk to someone to sort out your feelings as well as figure out how best to help your child. This may be a professional counselor, a member of the clergy, a family member, or a friend. Al-Anon (see *Organizations* on page 156), a support group for family members of problem drinkers, may also be helpful.

MAINTAIN A NORMAL ATMOSPHERE AT HOME. While your child's substance abuse may place seemingly unbearable strains on your family, try to keep your family life on an even keel, provide support and attention to your other children, and include your substance-abusing child in your family activities.

Doing Your Part to Discourage Drinking and Driving

Driving under the influence of either alcohol or drugs is illegal in all fifty states—and for good reason. It is a major health and safety problem. Car accidents in which one of the drivers is impaired is the single leading cause of death of American teenagers. The following are steps you can take to minimize the risk of your child driving while under the influence of drugs or alcohol:

HELP YOUR CHILD UNDERSTAND THE CONSEQUENCES OF DRIVING WHILE IMPAIRED. Review with him the statistics about car accidents resulting from drivers under the influence. Also talk with him about other consequences, including the likely loss of his license. Make sure he understands that you are telling him this because you want to make sure he is safe, not because you want to control him. Consider having this discussion with him while he is learning to drive so he sees it as part of the learning process rather than a lecture to be resisted.

Set Out Clear Rules About Drinking and Driving. These might include the following:

- Under no circumstances is he to drive while under the influence of drugs or alcohol.
- Drugs and alcohol are not allowed in the car at any time.
- He is not to get in a car with a driver who has been drinking or using drugs. Make it clear that he can call you for a ride at any time.

Coordinate Your Rules with Other Parents. Get together with parents of your child's friends to try to reach a consensus that all teen parties or social gatherings will be substance-free and supervised by adults.

Sign the "Contract for Life." This contract was established by Students Against Destructive Decisions (SADD). It obligates teenagers to call a parent if they have no other way of getting a safe ride home and obligates the parent to provide a ride and postpone any discussion until at least the next day. This contract is described on SADD's website (www.saddonline.com).

Educate Your Child About Alternatives to Driving While Impaired. Tell him that if he is under the influence, he is to find an alternative way of getting home such as having a friend who is not impaired drive him, calling you or a neighbor, or getting a cab. Or he can stay overnight after letting you know. Let him know, however, that this advice in no way means that he has your permission to use drugs or alcohol.

Show Your Child the Real-Life Results of Driving While Impaired. Impress upon him the seriousness of this problem by showing him pictures of car accidents caused by drunken or drug-involved drivers. A website that does this with graphic and disturbing pictures is www.knology.net/~ricknet/dui.htm. You might also talk with your child about someone you know who was injured in an alcohol- or drug-related accident.

PRESENT SOME SCENARIOS TO YOUR CHILD. Give him some realistic situations and discuss how he might handle them. Here are a couple of examples:

- You are at a party and the person who drove you has had a couple of beers. When it's time to go home, the only person available is the one who brought you. He tells you that he can drive without any problem. What should you do?

- You drive over to pick up a friend on the way to a party. A few minutes after getting in your car he takes a couple of beers out of a bag, offers you one, and starts drinking the other. What should you do?

CHALLENGE MYTHS PUT FORWARD BY YOUR CHILD. He may try to get you to back off your rules about drinking and driving by giving you misleading or incorrect information. Refute his statements in a calm and respectful manner. If he tells you that alcohol takes time to affect a person because it must be digested like food, inform him that alcohol is absorbed directly into the bloodstream and affects the person almost immediately. If he tells you that a couple of beers won't affect his driving ability, inform him that people react differently to alcohol and that two beers may be enough to make his driving risky, especially if he has a small physique or is thin. If he tells you that beer or wine coolers won't affect him the way hard liquor will, inform him that any kind of alcohol can affect his driving.

ENCOURAGE THE SCHOOL TO SPONSOR AN AFTER-PROM PARTY. This will significantly lessen the chance that students will use alcohol or drugs the night of the prom and endanger themselves or others by driving while impaired.

HELP YOUR CHILD RECOGNIZE IMPAIRED DRIVERS. Talk with your child about the importance of avoiding other drivers who appear to be under the influence. Teach him the warning signs of an impaired driver: he may swerve off the road, tailgate, go through stop signs, respond slowly to traffic lights, speed up or slow down quickly, and drive at night with his headlights off.

Facts About Teen Smoking

- The American Cancer Society defines cigarette smoking this way: "drawing smoke, fire, and toxic substances into your lungs for the purpose of giving the body a dose of nicotine, a highly toxic and addictive drug."

- The nicotine in cigarettes is what leads to an addiction to smoking. It reaches the brain within eight seconds of inhaling and causes pleasurable feelings so that the smoker wants to continue smoking.

- Each year smoking kills more than 400,000 Americans, more than the number of deaths from AIDS, alcohol and drug abuse, automobile accidents, homicides, suicides, and fires combined.

- Smoking is the primary cause of heart and lung disease and is associated with various forms of cancer. It can also worsen problems with asthma, high blood pressure, and diabetes.

- Every time a person smokes a cigarette, he takes in at least forty-three cancer-causing substances.

- More than 3 million American teenagers smoke cigarettes and more than 1 million teenage males use smokeless tobacco. About one in three American teens smoke or use smokeless tobacco.

- Every day more than three thousand young people begin smoking. That adds up to more than 1 million new smokers every year.

- Cigarettes are easy for youths to obtain. Seventy-six percent of eighth graders reported in a survey that they could obtain cigarettes without much trouble.

- More than 5 million youths living today will die prematurely due to a smoking-related disease.

- About 70 percent of smokers age seventeen or less say they regret having started.

- The decision to smoke is almost always made during the teenage years. Teens who do not start smoking in high school are unlikely to start later on.

- Teens underestimate the addictive effects of nicotine. Three of four students who smoked in high school were still smoking five years later even though almost all had planned to quit.

- Teens who smoke are more likely than their nonsmoking peers to use alcohol, marijuana, and cocaine. In addition, teen smokers are more likely to engage in risky behavior, including not wearing seat belts, having sex at an early age, getting into fights, and carrying weapons.

- A recent study indicates that advertising plays an even greater role than peer pressure in influencing teens to smoke.

- On an encouraging note, smoking by teenagers has recently begun to decline.

SMOKING CAN CAUSE . . .

. . . *lung cancer.* Smoking may thicken the bronchial lining, which can also impair the ability of the lungs to oxygenate the blood, leading to emphysema. In addition, smoking may contribute to cancer of the bladder, pancreas, and kidneys.

. . . *throat cancer.* It can cause the throat lining to thicken and may also lead to gum disease and tooth loss.

. . . *heart disease.* Coronary heart disease is the leading cause of death in the United States. People who smoke a pack of cigarettes per day are more than twice as likely to have a heart attack as people who do not smoke.

. . . *respiratory problems.* These include coughing and wheezing. Smoking may also trigger asthma attacks.

. . . *shortness of breath.* Because smoking may lessen the oxygen available for a person's muscles, it can also lead to slowed reaction time, decreased coordination, and impaired athletic performance.

. . . *a decrease in stamina.* Smokers run more slowly and shorter distances than they would if they did not smoke.

. . . *a diminished sense of smell and taste.* Food may not taste as good as it used to.

. . . *bad breath.* Tobacco tar is released when smokers exhale.

. . . *hair and clothes to smell.* This may turn off other people.

. . . *teeth to yellow.* Fingers and fingernails may also start to yellow.

. . . *sexual problems.* Male smokers may have decreased sperm count while female smokers are prone to infertility.

. . . *premature wrinkling of the face.* This can happen within five years of a person's beginning to smoke.

How to Discourage Your Child from Smoking

On average, youths who smoke have their first cigarette at the age of thirteen. This means that you need to make your views about smoking clear to your child from an early age. The list below offers strategies to deter your child from taking up this habit:

- Educate yourself about the health effects of tobacco so you can educate your child.
- Let your child know that you find smoking objectionable, but do not be dictatorial in your insistence that he not smoke. Rather, talk with him about the risks of smoking, and then tell him that he is a responsible person and you trust he will make a wise decision.

- Set a good example. Children with parents who smoke are more likely to smoke themselves. If you smoke, try to quit. If you are unable or unwilling, try to avoid smoking in your child's presence. Let him know that quitting smoking is difficult and, if true, that you regret having started. Don't leave cigarettes around the house and, of course, don't offer him any.

- Consider prohibiting smoking in your home and car. This sends a strong message that you find smoking unacceptable and that you have a concern for the impact of secondhand smoke.

- Talk to your child at an early age about the hazards of smoking and reinforce this message during the middle and high school years. Kids may begin experimenting with smoking as early as eleven. Let him know about the appearance problems associated with smoking, including bad breath, stained teeth, yellowed fingers, smelly clothes and hair, lessened stamina, decreased athletic performance, and facial wrinkles. He is likely to be more impressed with these cosmetic concerns than the serious physical consequences of smoking.

- If you smoke, be careful about sharing the serious physical problems associated with smoking with your child, especially if he is young, lest he conclude that you are going to die prematurely.

- Appeal to your child's desire for independence and control by telling him that nicotine is highly addictive so that once he starts smoking, he may find that he cannot stop.

- Help your child learn how to resist peer pressure to smoke. If he is receptive, try role-playing situations where he is offered cigarettes and suggest responses he can give to his peers.

- Let your child know that tobacco alternatives such as smokeless tobacco, cigars, and low-tar and additive-free cigarettes are not free of risk. All tobacco products contain nicotine.

- Do not let your child play with candy cigarettes. They may convey the message that cigarettes are pleasurable.

- Talk with your child about the price of smoking. Let him know that smoking costs on average about $700 a year. Give him some examples of what he could do with that money instead, such as purchase more than fifty CDs.

- Talk with your older children about how they are role models and that their smoking may influence their siblings to start.

- Discuss tobacco advertising with your child. Help him appreciate how tobacco companies target children with their ads by making it seem as if smoking is "cool" and everybody does it. Similarly, talk with him about how movies and magazines falsely depict smoking as a glamorous and sophisticated activity.

- Find out if the health curriculum at your child's school has an antismoking component. If not, suggest that it be included.

- Advocate for your child's school to make school events such as dances and sporting events tobacco-free.

- Try to go to restaurants that are completely nonsmoking. This will let your child know that you are serious about your objections to smoking.

Challenging Teens' Views About Smoking

Your child may justify smoking by making some misleading arguments, examples of which are described below. Help him separate smoking fact from fiction.

"OTHER KIDS THINK THAT SMOKING IS 'COOL.'" According to recent statistics and the "Surgeon General's Report on Kids' Smoking," it is only true if the "other kids" are teens who are unlikely to do well in school, who are prone to drug use, who often lack the confidence to say no when a peer offers them a cigarette, and who are more likely to engage in risky behavior such as fighting or having unprotected sex.

"SMOKING MAKES KIDS LOOK MORE GROWN UP." Grown up, maybe; appealing, unlikely. Smoking was considered a "dirty habit" by 72 percent of high school students in a recent survey. A similar percentage of teens said they would prefer to date someone who did not smoke.

"MOST KIDS MY AGE SMOKE." Not so. Tell your child that the majority of teenagers do not smoke.

"IF SMOKING GETS TO BE A PROBLEM FOR ME, I'LL JUST QUIT." As statistics show, this is not so simple. Most teens who smoke regularly become addicted to nicotine, making quitting a real challenge. Forty percent of teen smokers reported in a survey that they tried to quit but could not.

"IF I ONLY SMOKE OCCASIONALLY, IT WON'T HURT ME." The Surgeon General says otherwise. He reports that teens who smoke just one cigarette a week will show symptoms of wheezing and coughing.

"THOSE PHYSICAL PROBLEMS WON'T HAPPEN TO ME UNTIL I'M A LOT OLDER." A teenager begins to experience physical symptoms—coughing, shortness of breath, nausea, and dizziness—soon after having his first cigarette.

"IT'S OKAY TO USE SMOKELESS TOBACCO BECAUSE IT IS SAFER THAN SMOKING CIGARETTES." The reality is that smokeless tobacco (also known as chewing or spit tobacco or snuff) is very harmful. It can cause bleeding gums, mouth sores that don't heal, and cancer.

Helping Your Child Quit Smoking

Quitting smoking is a daunting challenge, but one that is easier if your child has your emotional support and practical assistance. While he may need the support of a smoking cessation program, he may also benefit from the following strategies:

- Educate your child about the risks of smoking, both short- and long-term. If necessary, provide him with antismoking materials.

- Have your child make a list of the pros and cons of smoking. Have him divide a sheet in half and list the reasons to smoke on one side and the reasons not to smoke on the other. You may want to help him come up with reasons for not smoking.

- Encourage your child to stop smoking without being confrontational. Be supportive and understanding, and let him know that you will help him if he makes the decision to quit.

- If you smoke, offer to stop with him, if possible, and then work out a specific plan for quitting.

- If your child decides to quit, support him by not smoking in his presence. Hide your cigarettes from him and remove ashtrays from the house. Avoid taking him to places where people smoke. Try to go to smoke-free restaurants.

- Have him check out the website www.quitnet.org to get support and ideas from others who are trying to quit.

- Suggest that your child attend Nicotine Anonymous meetings. Similar to Alcoholics Anonymous, this organization offers support and practical guidance. Go to its website (www.nicotine-anonymous.org) to find a chapter near you.

- Help your child find an antismoking program that he can join. Local chapters of the American Cancer Society, the American Lung Association, or the American Heart Association may run programs. Find out if there is a program that caters to teens. Your child's physician may be able to help you find one.

- Keep in mind that there are various methods of quitting and a range of antismoking aids, including a nicotine patch, a nicotine inhaler, nicotine gum, sugarless gum, medication such as Zyban, cinnamon sticks, and aversion therapy. Some of these require a prescription from a physician.

- The following are some tips that may help your child quit smoking:

- Avoid alcohol, sugar, and coffee during the initial weeks after quitting because they stimulate the desire for a cigarette.
- Be disciplined about your diet to avoid gaining weight.
- Snack on low-calorie foods such as celery, carrots, and apples.
- Eat slowly, taking time between bites.
- Chew on cinnamon sticks, which can be purchased in any supermarket.
- Build exercise into your daily routine.
- Take a yoga class to help you learn how to relax and relieve stress.
- Learn how to do deep breathing. If you are feeling the temptation to smoke, deep breathing can help the urge to pass.
- Let your friends know you are quitting and ask for their tolerance if you are irritable.

RECOMMENDED READING

Books for Kids

Aaseng, N. (2000). *Teens and Drunk Driving.* San Diego, CA: Lucent Books (grades 6-9).

Ayer, E. H. (1998). *Teen Smoking.* San Diego, CA: Lucent Books (grades 4-12).

Bichler, C. (1999). *Teen Drinking.* New York: Rosen Publishing Group (grades 7-12).

Mass, W. (1997). *Teen Drug Abuse.* San Diego, CA: Lucent Books (grades 4-12).

Moe, B. A. (2000). *Teen Smoking and Tobacco Use: A Hot Issue.* Springfield, NJ: Enslow Publishers (grades 6 and up).

Books for Parents

Babbit, N. (2000). *Adolescent Drug and Alcohol Abuse: How to Spot It, Stop It, and Get Help for Your Family.* Sebastopol, CA: O'Reilly & Associates.

Newton, C. (2001). *Generation Risk: How to Protect Your Child from Smoking and Other Dangerous Behavior.* New York: M. Evans and Company.

Tobias, J. M. (1989). *Kids and Drugs: A Handbook for Parents and Professionals* (2nd ed.). Annandale, VA: Panda Press.

ORGANIZATIONS

Al-Anon/Alateen Family Groups

1600 Corporate Landing Parkway
Virginia Beach, VA 23454-5617
1-888-4AL-ANON
www.al-anon.alateen.org

Al-Anon provides hope and help to families and friends who are dealing with the drinking problem of a relative or friend. Alateen is a program for young people dealing with the same issues.

Alcoholics Anonymous

475 Riverside Drive, 11th floor
New York, NY 10115
1-212-870-3400
www.aa.org

A group of individuals who meet regularly with the goals of stopping drinking and maintaining their sobriety. Members share their experiences and provide each other with support, strength, and hope.

Mothers Against Drunk Driving (MADD)

511 East John Carpenter Freeway, Suite 700
Irving, TX 75062
1-214-744-6233
www.madd.org

With more than 600 chapters nationwide, MADD works to find effective solutions to the problems of drunk driving and under-age drinking while supporting the victims of drunk driving.

National Clearinghouse for Alcohol and Drug Information

P. O. Box 2345
Rockville, MD 20847-2345
1-800-729-6686
www.health.org

A federal organization that distributes substance-abuse prevention and treatment information to the general public and also provides treatment referrals.

National Commission Against Drunk Driving

1900 L Street, NW, Suite 705
Washington, DC 20036
1-202-452-6004
www.ncadd.com

Identifies strategies and programs that show promise in reducing the number of people who drive while impaired.

Stop Teenage Addiction to Tobacco

Northeastern University
360 Huntington Avenue
241 Cushing Hall
Boston, MA 02115
1-617-373-7828
www.stat.org

This national organization's mission is to end childhood and teenage addiction to tobacco.

Students Against Destructive Decisions (SADD)

P. O. Box 800
Marlboro, MA 01752
1-800-787-5777
www.saddonline.com

Formerly called Students Against Drunk Driving. Provides students with the tools to deal with the issues of under-age drinking, drunk driving, drug abuse, and other destructive decisions.

CHAPTER 8

Protecting Your Child from Sexual Predators

Jill's relationship with her mother's boyfriend, Ray, began very innocently. He would take her to her favorite restaurants, play games with her, watch television with her, and play tickling games with her. He made her feel special. He had promised that for her eighth birthday he would take her out for a special day— just the two of them. Ray's interest in Jill continued until Jill's mother began to grow concerned and confused. She didn't understand why her boyfriend was spending as much time with Jill as he was with her. She wasn't quite sure why, but her instincts told her that Ray's interest in her daughter was inappropriate.

Her concern mounted as she began to notice some puzzling changes in Jill's behavior. Jill began to wet her bed and was even starting to suck her thumb again. She seemed distant and sometimes lost in her own world. Her mother also noticed that Jill began to cling to her when Ray was around. Soon after these changes became evident, Jill approached her mother, claiming to be upset for her friend who Jill said was being made to do things by her friend's brother that she didn't like. Jill wanted to know what she should do. Sensing that Jill was not really inquiring about her girlfriend but about herself, her mother asked some questions. Eventually the truth emerged: Ray was sexually abusing Jill.

What Ray did to Jill was not only a betrayal of her trust and a violation of her body, it was also a crime. And, sadly, it is a pervasive problem in our society. Children are sexually abused at an alarming rate. It is estimated that one in five girls and one in seven boys are sexually abused before turning eighteen.

What exactly is child sexual abuse? It is an act that occurs when an adult or older child uses a child to obtain sexual pleasure. The activity need not involve sexual contact. As with any form of abuse, sexual abuse can be physical, verbal, or emotional. It can be so subtle that a child may not understand what is happening other than knowing that she is uncomfortable. Sexual abuse can consist of a single incident or multiple acts over a prolonged period. Children of any age can be victims of sexual abuse.

People who sexually abuse children use their power and authority over children to exploit their innocence and vulnerability. They know how hard it is for children to say no to adults or question their authority. They take advantage of children's desire to please. They play on their emotions. They may trick them, bribe them, coax them, pressure them, threaten them, and sometimes even force them to give them what they want: sexual gratification.

Children who have been sexually abused have been called "the silent children," and for good reason. Many children who are sexually abused keep quiet about it. They may feel embarrassed about what happened, guilty that they did something wrong, and fearful of what the abuser will do if they tell. This makes the identification of sexual abuse a very difficult job. Often the only way it is known is by the child's own disclosure.

Parents play a critical role in protecting their children from sexual abuse. We have laws intended to protect children from sexual abuse (including laws requiring that residents be notified if a sex offender has moved into the community), and some schools offer education about ways of staying safe, but parents hold the key to safeguarding their children. The challenge is to provide children with the knowledge and tools to stay safe while not frightening them or teaching them to mistrust others.

The parents' job does not end with teaching their children some safety lessons. They also need to be alert to people who are acting inappropriately with children, who should not have to shoulder the responsibility for preventing sexual abuse. Adults must assume the primary burden for protecting children.

What You Need to Know About Sexual Abuse

- Experts estimate that there are 60 million people in America who were sexually abused as children.

- Children with disabilities are estimated to be four to ten times more likely to be sexually abused than their nondisabled peers.

- Sexual abuse is never the fault of the child.

- Most children who are victims of sexual abuse do not tell anybody what happened to them.

- Most incidents of sexual abuse—estimates range from 70 percent to 85 percent—are committed by someone a child knows. Children are more likely to be preyed upon by relatives, friends, neighbors, or caretakers than strangers lurking on the edges of playgrounds and parks.

- Sexual offenders can come from any cultural and socioeconomic background.

- The impact of sexual abuse on the child depends in large part on the response of the family.

CHILD SEXUAL ABUSE CAN INCLUDE . . .

. . . sexual touching or fondling.

. . . dating violence.

. . . forcing a child to pose, undress, or perform sexual acts on film or in person.

. . . making threats to a child to force her to engage in sexual activity.

. . . making offensive or insulting remarks of a sexual nature.

. . . exposing a child to a person's genitals, adult sexual acts, or pornography.

. . . watching a child undress, often without her knowledge.

Sexual Abuse Myths

Families that are grappling with the trauma of sexual abuse need to be cautious about automatically believing what they hear, because they are likely to have to contend with false or misleading statements that may cause them further worry or distress. Here are some common myths about child sexual abuse:

"CHILDREN OFTEN FABRICATE STORIES OF SEXUAL ABUSE." Children do make up tales, but rarely do they lie about sexual abuse. Children who initiate a report that they have been sexually abused often describe sexual behavior in detail, information they are unlikely to have unless their stories are true.

"CHILDREN ARE MOST OFTEN SEXUALLY ABUSED BY STRANGERS." The reality is that most children know the people who abuse them.

"SEXUAL ABUSERS HAVE A SLEAZY OR FRIGHTENING APPEARANCE." In fact, sexual abusers do not look any different from anyone else.

"IF THE CHILD DOES NOT COMPLAIN OR SHOW DISTRESS DURING THE SEXUAL ACTIVITY, THEN IT IS NOT REALLY ABUSE."

This is a particularly harmful myth. The child's silence may reflect her fear of saying something and does not mean that she is not feeling upset or scared. Indeed, she may be overwhelmed with emotion. Even if she responds physically to the sexual activity, it is no less of an abusive act. In the case of a young child, she is not likely to have the knowledge or emotional tools to understand what the person has done to her or that it was wrong. Nonetheless, it is still abuse.

"THE CHILD IS AT FAULT FOR ENCOURAGING THE SEXUAL ACTIVITY." Absolutely not. A child cannot be held responsible for the behavior of an adult. The child is in a vulnerable position relative to the adult, who often has authority over her and may use this power to manipulate her. She is likely to trust the person and may be afraid of disappointing or alienating that person. It is very hard for children to say no to adults.

"CHILDREN WHO ARE SEXUALLY ABUSED ARE SCARRED FOREVER." While being sexually abused can be a traumatic situation that a child never forgets, it need not damage her for the rest of her life. Many victims, with guidance and support, do heal with time and go on to lead normal, happy lives. In addition, sexual abuse does not leave any permanent physical marks.

"IF YOU AND YOUR CHILD DO NOT TALK ABOUT THE SEXUAL ABUSE, IT WILL EVENTUALLY GO AWAY." A child who has experienced ongoing sexual abuse will experience a range of powerful emotions that are unlikely to go away without parental guidance and perhaps professional help. Indeed, without help, the emotional pain and guilt resulting from the abuse may hamper her development in later years. It is the emotional equivalent of neglecting an open wound.

Characteristics of a Sexual Predator

While there is no such thing as a "typical" child sexual predator, the following generalizations can be made:

- Sexual predators come from all walks of life and all racial, ethnic, and socioeconomic backgrounds.

- Most sexual predators are heterosexual males.

- Many sexual predators are under the age of eighteen.

- They are typically sexually attracted to children and seek sexual gratification through their contact with them.

- A sexual predator is known to the child in most cases. He can be a family member, a family friend, a neighbor, a coach, a teacher, a caretaker, or anyone else who is involved with the child.

- A sexual predator may spend weeks or even months cultivating his relationship with the child.

- A predator may bribe children with toys or sweets in an effort to seduce them.

- Pedators may produce or collect child pornography.

Behaviors That Warrant Concern

Adults who are involved with your child may behave toward her in a way that raises your concern. If you continue to feel uncomfortable, talk with the person, making sure to use discretion. You need peace of mind that your child is being treated appropriately. Close monitoring may be needed if a person:

- pays an unusual amount of attention to your child.

- seeks out opportunities to spend uninterrupted time alone with your child.

- frequently buys expensive gifts for your child or gives her money.

- often walks into the bathroom while your child is there.

- shows unusual interest in the sexuality of your child (for example, he may make inappropriate references to her body).

- pursues physical contact with your child through hugging, touching, tickling, or wrestling even when she has indicated that she does not like it.

- spends most of his free time with children rather than with persons his age.

- asks to take your child on overnight trips alone.

- frequently offers to care for children for free.

- asks that your child keep secrets.

What You Can Do to Protect Your Child

While we cannot completely protect our children from sexual abuse, we can take steps to lessen the chance that it happens. One of your key tasks is to create a climate in which your child feels comfortable being open with you about sensitive matters. The list below offers some guidelines for keeping your child safe and giving her the knowledge and tools to make good decisions. This is a delicate task. You want to teach your child to be vigilant, but you don't want to scare her or cause her to mistrust all adults.

- Teach your child that sometimes adults will make children do things that are uncomfortable and then ask that they keep it a secret. Tell her that if any person asks her to keep a secret, she should tell you immediately.

- Teach your child the difference between "good" and "bad" touching, the difference between affection and abuse. Let her know that no one has the right to hurt her or touch her in her private areas. (If necessary you can tell her that these are the parts of the body covered by a bathing suit.)

- Teach your child the names of body parts so that if somebody touches her inappropriately, she can describe to you precisely what happened and also feel comfortable talking to you about her concerns.

- Teach your child that it is okay to say no. In teaching your child to be polite and respectful to grown-ups, make it clear that being polite does not mean she should do something that she feels is wrong if a grown-up tells her to. Let her know that if someone wants her to do something that will make her feel uncomfortable or that she feels is wrong, even if the person is a relative or family friend, she can say no, and she should tell you about it.

- You might role-play with your child. Pose some situations to her and ask what she would do. (For example, "What would you do if someone asked you to come into his house to see his new dog?") If she is not sure, offer suggestions about what she can do or say.

- Teach your child to tell you if someone has done something to hurt her or make her feel uncomfortable, such as touching her, asking her to touch him, or trying to get her to undress. Reassure her that you will do everything in your power to protect her. Tell her she will not get in trouble for telling or be blamed for what happened to her.

- Teach your child that she is not to play secret games with anyone, especially with adults. Tell her she should let you know if an adult suggests playing such a game with her.

- Teach your younger child that she should never go into anyone's home without you—no matter who it is—unless she has your permission. An older child can be given more leeway.

- Tell your child that she should never accept a ride from anyone unless you have told her in advance that the person would be picking her up.

- Tell your child she is not to accept gifts or treats from a stranger when she is not with you.

- Teach your child to yell "No" or "Get away from me" if a stranger tries to grab her or is clearly following her, then run to a place where there are other people and tell a trusted adult.

○ Exercise caution when choosing someone to care for your child. Meet the caregiver, interview her, observe her interactions with your child, and check her references. (See chapter 1 for more on child care safety.)

○ Pay careful attention if your child is very resistant to being left alone with a particular person. Ask her why she doesn't want to be with that person.

Why Children Don't Tell

Sexual abuse has often been called "the silent problem" because children are very reluctant to reveal that they have been sexually abused. Their silence, however, protects the abuser and allows the abuse to continue. Children might keep quiet about what is happening to them because they may:

○ not understand what happened to them or appreciate that what was done to them was wrong.

○ be unable to put it into words.

○ be uncomfortable talking about sexual issues.

○ convince themselves that it will not happen again.

○ believe that it happens to many other children.

○ assume that no one will believe them.

○ feel guilty that they have done something bad and are too ashamed or embarrassed to let anybody know.

○ be afraid they will be blamed for the abuse and punished for their behavior.

○ be frightened that everybody will find out what happened and reject or shun them.

- be fearful of disappointing their parents and being rejected by them.

- be afraid that they or their family will be hurt as a result of threats from the abuser.

- be terrified that they will be sent away.

- be scared of getting the person who abused them in trouble.

- fear losing the attention and affection of someone they love.

- dread having to answer many questions.

- fear that they will have to go to court.

When Children Are More Likely to Tell

Although sexual abuse is very awkward and embarrassing for a child to talk about, she may be more willing to tell her parents about an incident if they have previously discussed with her "good" and "bad" touching, and encouraged her to say no and tell them if someone wanted her to do something that made her feel uncomfortable. Children may be prompted to tell their parents about an incident of sexual abuse if they:

- are confident that someone will put an end to the abuse and protect them.

- believe there is someone they can tell who will be accepting and nonjudgmental.

- feel they will be believed and their distress taken seriously.

- feel they will not be blamed for the abuse.

- learn that there is someone who is aware of the abuse.

- are concerned about the welfare of another child who is being abused.

- learn that something can be done to stop the abuse.

- suffer a physical injury.

- feel overwhelmed by the emotional pain.
- are pregnant or fearful of becoming pregnant.

Physical Signs Suggesting Sexual Abuse

Sexual abuse may cause physical injury to a child. The following is a list of physical signs that warrant your attention and follow-up. If you observe one or more of these indicators, consider having your child examined by a physician who has experience in treating children victimized by sexual abuse.

- Pregnancy
- Sexually transmitted disease
- Pain, bleeding, or discharge in the genital or anal area
- Unexplained scratches, bruises, rashes, redness or swelling, particularly in the genital or anal area
- Pain while urinating or defecating
- Unexplained stomachaches or headaches
- Discomfort when sitting or walking
- Torn clothing
- Blood or discharge on bedsheets or clothing, especially underwear
- Significant change in appetite, with weight gain or loss
- Sleep disturbances such as insomnia, nightmares, or bed-wetting
- Excessive masturbation

Behavioral Signs Suggesting Sexual Abuse

Children who have been sexually abused rarely speak directly of their abuse, but they may communicate it indirectly through their behavior. The following is a list of behaviors that may signal that sexual abuse has occurred. It is important to bear in mind that no one behavior should be interpreted to mean that abuse has taken place. If you observe a pattern of these behaviors, however, you will want to ask your child some questions in a gentle and supportive manner, making sure to avoid grilling her or asking leading questions. Caution is warranted here lest you be overzealous in identifying sexual abuse. But if your instincts tell you that something is wrong, you're probably right. Keep in mind that some of these behaviors may arise from causes other than sexual abuse, including divorce, the death or illness of a family member, or peer problems.

- Suggestions from the child that something is amiss, ranging from direct statements ("The babysitter played a touching game with me, and I didn't like it") to indirect clues ("I really don't want that babysitter") to disguised revelations ("My friend's brother keeps doing things to her that she doesn't like. What should I tell her?").

- Uncharacteristic immature, babyish behavior such as thumb sucking, bedwetting, whining, or clinginess

- Fear of being alone or being in the dark

- Lack of affect or expressiveness

- Uncharacteristic sadness

- Frequent crying episodes

- Unusual irritability, anger, or aggression

- Tendency to space out or withdraw into a fantasy world

- Self-destructive behavior, such as an older child engaging in drug or alcohol abuse, burning or cutting herself, or suicide attempts

- Running away

- Withdrawal from family and peers

- Preoccupation with sexual matters, as reflected in her play, drawings, stories, and conversations

- Advanced sexual knowledge and language for her age

- Promiscuous or seductive behavior

- Inappropriate physical contact with children or adults

- Sexual abuse of other children

- Reluctance to be with a certain person or go to a particular place

- Dramatic decline in school performance, including truancy, decrease in grades, or lack of concentration

- Dressing and acting too old for her age, such as wearing make-up at a young age or dressing in tight or revealing clothing

- Wearing an excessive amount of clothing, such as dressing in many layers

- Changes in hygiene habits, such as excessive cleanliness or lack of cleanliness

- Lack of interest in activities that previously held her interest

How a Child Who Has Been Sexually Abused Might Feel

A sexually abused child may experience a wide range of emotions in the aftermath of the abuse. Some of these feelings may be overwhelming. The depth of the child's reactions may depend on her age and her cognitive and emotional development. Further, the responses of important people in her life will have a strong impact on how quickly and how fully she recovers from the abuse. A child whose parents are supportive, reassuring, and strong will fare much better than one whose parents withdraw or seem unable to cope with the problem. Parents of sexual abuse victims might also experience some of the feelings that the child does.

A CHILD WHO HAS BEEN THE VICTIM OF SEXUAL ABUSE MIGHT FEEL . . .

. . . *overwhelmed* by the rush of emotions she is experiencing.

. . . *angry* at the person who abused her.

. . . *angry* at the people she perceives did not protect her.

. . . *angry* at herself for allowing it to go on.

. . . *fearful* that her parents will be angry or disappointed with her.

. . . *fearful* that the person who abused her will harm her or her family because she told someone.

. . . *fearful* that she will cause problems for the abuser for whom she may still have some affection.

. . . *fearful* that her peers will reject her.

. . . *fearful* that she may be taken away from her home.

. . . *hurt* that someone she trusted would do this to her.

. . . *guilty* because she thinks she has done something wrong. She may have difficulty distinguishing between "I did something wrong" and "Someone did something wrong to me."

. . . *guilty* for participating in the abuse, especially if it went on for a long time.

. . . *guilty* if she broke a parental rule while the abuse went on.

. . . *ashamed* if she experienced some pleasure from the sexual contact. She might say to herself, "I must be bad because it felt good."

. . . *confused* because she may still have feelings of affection for her abuser even though he did something very wrong to her.

. . . *confused* that an adult whom she trusted did something to her that was against the law.

. . . *worthless*, thinking that something is wrong with her in the eyes of others and in her own eyes because she has been violated. She may feel that no one will want her for a friend.

. . . *uncomfortable* with physical contact. Being touched may remind her of the abuse and cause her to avoid physical contact.

. . . *alone* because she may feel that others cannot understand what she experienced and what she is feeling.

. . . *numb* due to the overwhelming pain and hurt. She may try to minimize the experience by pretending that it did not occur.

What to Do if Your Child Has Been Sexually Abused

If your child trusts you enough to tell you that she has been sexually abused, you can play a significant role in helping her cope with what is likely a traumatic situation for her. Keep in mind that your *initial* response to her disclosure is particularly important in conveying support and understanding. In turn, it is important that you obtain the emotional and practical support of others, such as friends, relatives, or a counselor. The following are stra-tegies for providing your child with support and guidance.

REMAIN CALM. As upset and angry as you no doubt will be upon finding out that your child has been sexually abused, try to contain your emotions. Your child may be frightened by your reaction and may mistakenly conclude that you are angry with her. If so, reassure her that you are in no way upset with her. Give her confidence that you are strong enough emotionally to help and protect her.

PROVIDE SUPPORT AND COMFORT. Your child has been through a very emotional ordeal and needs your care and concern as well as your expression of love. Responding in this way will help reestablish her trust in adults. Reassure her that she is not alone and that what happened to her has happened to other children.

COMMEND YOUR CHILD FOR TELLING YOU WHAT HAPPENED. It may have taken considerable courage for your child to tell you what happened. She may have feared your reaction and what the person who abused her might do to her for telling. Emphasize that she did the right thing by letting you know and tell her that you understand it was hard for her to do this.

LET YOUR CHILD KNOW THAT YOU BELIEVE HER. It is unusual for a child to lie about sexual abuse, especially because of the embarrassment of talking about it.

REASSURE YOUR CHILD THAT YOU WILL PROTECT HER. She needs to know that you will do everything possible to see that the abuse stops and keep her safe. Reassure her that you will not let the person who abused her do anything to her because she told on him.

TELL YOUR CHILD THAT SHE HAS DONE NOTHING WRONG. She may feel that she is to blame for what happened and that she is a bad person. Help her overcome these feelings by telling her, for example, "I know you couldn't help it. You did absolutely nothing wrong." Let her know that her abuser was very wrong to do what he did and that she is not responsible for his behavior.

BE HONEST WITH YOUR CHILD. Answer her questions as well as you can. If you do not know the answer, say so. Do not make promises that you cannot keep. If she has been hurt and she wants you to keep it a secret, you must let her know that you must report the abuse (while also informing her that this will help protect her).

LISTEN ATTENTIVELY. Be patient as she describes to you what happened. It is not easy for her to do this. Acknowledge what she is feeling and how difficult it is to talk about it. Let her talk at her own pace without pressure from you to give more details. You might say to her, "Use your own words and take as much time as you need." A child who feels listened to and understood is likely to make a better adjustment after the sexual abuse.

RESPECT YOUR CHILD'S PRIVACY. Talk with your child about the abuse in a private place where no one else is present. She will likely be very concerned that others will find out what happened. Reassure her that you will only talk about it with others who must know about it to help protect and support her.

ALLOW YOUR CHILD TO EXPRESS HER EMOTIONS, EVEN IF THEY ARE EXTREME. She may experience swings of emotion, from sadness to rage. While it is very hard to see your child in pain, recognize that you cannot simply turn off her feelings or make her pain go away. Try to stay calm and accepting of her emotional expressions. You might even give her a pillow she can punch if she is angry. However, allowing her to vent does not mean that you have to accept inappropriate behavior or physical aggression toward you or others.

CONSIDER GOING TO A CRISIS CENTER OR CONTACTING AN ABUSE HOTLINE if you need immediate help.

OBTAIN MEDICAL HELP from a doctor who is trained in identifying and treating sexual abuse. Your child's regular doctor, a crisis center, or a children's hospital may be able to refer you to a doctor with this experience. The physician can determine whether your child has suffered any physical injury, obtain evidence of the abuse, and provide some reassurance to her that she has suffered no permanent injury.

OBTAIN COUNSELING FOR YOUR CHILD. Do not assume that the problem will go away on its own. Try to find a counselor trained in working with children who have been sexually abused. A crisis center or sexual assault center will be able to refer you to counselors with this experience. The counselor will meet with your child and perhaps other family members to determine whether she and your family need professional help. Counseling will be especially important if the abuse was inflicted by a family member, if it occurred over a long period of time, or if your child is showing behavioral signs of distress. Counselors can help your child to:

- express her emotions openly.

- understand that she is not to blame for the abuse and has no reason to feel guilty.

- feel a greater sense of self-worth.

- modify "acting out" or inappropriate behavior that she is exhibiting.

- resume her normal routines and activities.

- know what to do in the future to prevent other acts of sexual abuse.

INFORM THE APPROPRIATE STATE AGENCY. The agency responsible for child protection can help protect your child and guide you in what steps to take next, including informing law enforcement officials. Contact this agency rather than confronting the person you suspect of abuse or going to the place where it happened.

WRITE DOWN WHAT YOUR CHILD TELLS YOU. When you have finished talking with her, record what she has said, using her words as much as possible and avoiding interpreting or reading into what she has said. Be as specific as possible.

REMAIN AVAILABLE TO YOUR CHILD. A child's trust in adults is often a casualty of sexual abuse, so you will need to reestablish her trust in adults. You can do this by keeping open the lines of communication so she will be comfortable telling you about her concerns. Let her know she can come to you at any time to discuss anything she wants.

RETURN TO A NORMAL ROUTINE AT HOME AS SOON AS YOU CAN. Expecting your child to return to following your rules at home and doing her assigned chores as well as resuming normal family activities may sound insensitive, but it will help reestablish a familiar structure and make her feel more secure and stable. Of course, you may need to adjust your expectations and rules based on her adjustment.

BE SENSITIVE TO YOUR OTHER CHILDREN. Consider telling them what happened. If you do, provide information that is appropriate to their age and avoid sharing intimate details. They may fear they will suffer the same fate, so give them some basic strategies for protecting themselves. At the same time, reassure them that you will do everything in your power to make sure they are safe. Also give them the same love and caring you are giving to your child who was abused.

REEXAMINE YOUR BEHAVIOR WITH YOUR CHILDREN. You may need to modify how you respond to them in the aftermath of the sexual abuse because of the abused child's increased sensitivity. For example, you might establish or reinforce a household rule that everyone (including the parents) must knock when a bedroom or bathroom door is closed. You might also avoid wearing revealing clothing (for example, just underwear) outside the bedroom and having your child in bed with you. Be cautious about wrestling with or tickling your child in light of her possible sensitivity about touching. These kinds of rules will help provide the structure, comfort, and security that all children need to grow into healthy adults.

CONSIDER GETTING PROFESSIONAL HELP FOR YOURSELF. Finding out that your child has been sexually abused can be devastating. You may need support to help you deal with your own feelings, to know how to respond to her, and to mobilize the strength to give her support.

ALLOW TIME FOR HEALING. Recognize that your child's recovery is a slow process that cannot be rushed.

What You Should Not Do if Your Child Has Been Sexually Abused

- Do not panic upon hearing of the sexual abuse.
- Do not blame your child, criticize her, or get angry at her. And certainly do not punish her.

- Do not challenge your child by asking such questions as "Why did you wait so long to tell me?" or "Why didn't you run away?"

- Do not suggest to your child what may have happened by using leading questions or putting words in her mouth.

- Do not lie to your child or make promises you cannot keep.

- Do not pressure your child to talk about or give you further details of the abuse.

- Do not prevent your child from talking about the abuse if she wants to in the hope that she will forget about it.

- Do not talk about the sexual abuse constantly in the presence of your child.

- Do not confront your child's abuser in her presence.

RECOMMENDED READING

Books for Kids

Girard, L.W. (1987). *My Body Is Private.* Morton Grove, IL: Albert Whitman & Co. (ages 4-8).

Gordon, S. (1992). *Better Safe Than Sorry Book: A Family Guide for Sexual Assault Prevention.* Amherst, NY: Prometheus (ages 4-8).

Johnsen, K. (1992). *The Trouble with Secrets.* Seattle, WA: Parenting Press (ages 4-8).

Kleven, S. (1998). *The Right Touch: A Read-Aloud Story to Help Prevent Child Sexual Abuse.* Bellevue, WA: Illumination Arts (ages 4-8).

Books for Parents

Adams, C., and Fay, J. (1992). *Helping Your Child Recover from Sexual Abuse.* Seattle, WA: University of Washington Press.

Mahoney, D. (1999). *Innocence Lost: Protecting Your Child from the Trauma of Abuse.* Emeryville, CA: West Coast Media Group.

Mains, K. B., and Hancock, M. (1997). *Child Sexual Abuse: A Hope for Healing* (2nd ed.). Wheaton, IL: Harold Shaw Publications.

Monahon, C. (1997). *Children and Trauma: A Parent's Guide to Helping Children Heal.* San Francisco: Jossey-Bass.

Wooden, K. (1995). *Child Lures: What Every Parent and Child Should Know About Preventing Sexual Assault and Abduction.* Sarasota, FL: Book World.

ORGANIZATIONS

Mothers Against Sexual Abuse (MASA)

503 1/2 South Myrtle Avenue, #9
Monrovia, CA 91016
1-626-305-1986
www.againstsexualabuse.org

A national organization that educates the public about child sexual abuse, supports legislation to protect children, and provides referrals to help victims of sexual abuse and their families.

Red Flag Green Flag Resources

P. O. Box 2984
Fargo, ND 58108-2984
1-800-627-3675
www.redflaggreenflag.com

Publication division of the Rape and Abuse Crisis Center. It offers workbooks and videos for children, adolescents, and adults about child sexual abuse, domestic violence, and sexual assault.

Safeguarding Our Children–United Mothers

1852 West 11th Street, #191
Tracy, CA 95376
1-209-832-5703
www.soc-um.org

Promotes public awareness and prevention of child sexual abuse. A resource to those who have been sexually abused and their families.

The Safer Society Foundation

P. O. Box 340
Brandon, VT 05733-0340
1-802-247-3132
www.safersociety.com

A national research, advocacy, and referral center for the prevention and treatment of sexual abuse.

STOP IT NOW!

P. O. Box 495
Haydenville, MA 01039
1-413-268-3096
www.stopitnow.com

Works to increase public awareness of child sexual abuse, educate adults about ways to stop sexual abuse, and encourage abusers and potential abusers to seek help.

Survivors and Victims Empowered

P. O. Box 3030
Lancaster, PA 17604-3030
1-717-291-1940
www.s-a-v-e.org

Helps prevent the physical, emotional, and sexual abuse of children by raising public awareness and offering potential solutions.

Yellow Dyno

203 Barsana Avenue
Austin, TX 78737
1-512-288-2882
www.yellowdyno.com

Educates children on how to protect themselves from child abuse, abduction, and sexual molestation.

CHAPTER 9

Understanding and Preventing Teen Suicide

Kristen and Jason were inseparable. Dating since the ninth grade, they were the best of friends, spending most of their free time together. During the early part of tenth grade, Kristen's father died in a car accident. She was finding it extemely difficult to cope with her father's death. Her mother and older siblings did everything they could to provide Kristen with the emotional support she needed. They attended support groups together and looked for ways to draw her out of her grief. But it was Jason she looked to for emotional comfort, becoming increasingly dependent on him. As Kristen and Jason entered eleventh grade, their relationship soured. He was being pursued by another girl, and he was eager to go out with her. Kristen, already in a fragile emotional state, was devastated when Jason broke up with her. Time did little to heal her wound. She showed little interest in anything going on around her, whether at home or at school. She began to talk about how life wasn't worth living. Looking for a way to ease her seemingly intolerable pain, one Saturday evening Kristen put a gun to her head and ended her life.

Every year many teens make the same fateful decision Kristen made. In the United States an estimated five hundred thousand teenagers attempt suicide every year, and about five thousand succeed. The suicide or attempted suicide of a child can be earth-shattering to a family, rocking its very foundation.

Indeed, it is hard to imagine a more traumatic event for parents than the suicide of their child. In addition, friends, neighbors, and members of their community must also try to make sense of a seemingly senseless death.

It is hard to comprehend suicide, let alone teen suicide. Understanding adolescence gives only a partial answer. Being a teenager in today's world presents difficult challenges. It is a time of turmoil and stress as teens face dramatic changes. Their bodies are changing, they are forging new relationships, and they are grappling with decisions about their future. Insecurity and self-doubt may flourish. Teens vary in how they deal with these stresses, with some demonstrating better coping skills than others. Events that may appear insignificant to adults can often be crushing to a teenager. Some may find the stress insurmountable, leading to feelings of despair and hopelessness. Believing they have no one to turn to and looking for a solution to their pain, they may entertain thoughts of suicide.

When an emotionally fragile or depressed teen gives us warning signs that she is troubled, we need to take these signs seriously and give her support and professional help. Fortunately, depression is a problem that is treatable. Most children and teens who experience the despair and helplessness of depression can be helped. Because depressed teens are unlikely to seek help for themselves, parents often must take the initiative to obtain help for them.

Teen Suicide Facts

- Youth suicide rates have tripled in the past three decades. Suicide is the third leading cause of death for fifteen- to nineteen-year-olds.

- While younger children rarely commit suicide, there has been a dramatic increase in recent years in the suicide rate among ten- to fourteen-year-olds.

○ On average, one out of every three school districts loses a student to suicide yearly.

○ Almost twice as many teenagers die as a result of suicide than all natural causes combined.

○ For every teen who commits suicide, an estimated one hundred more will attempt it.

○ In a recent survey by the Centers for Disease Control, 24 percent of high school students had thought seriously about attempting suicide, 17 percent had made a specific plan to commit suicide, and 8 percent had actually attempted suicide.

○ Suicide is a very democratic problem, affecting individuals of all ages, races, and socioeconomic levels.

○ Girls are more likely to attempt suicide, while boys are more likely to actually commit suicide.

○ Approximately one third of all teenagers who attempt or commit suicide are gay or lesbian. Gay and lesbian youth are two to three times more likely to commit suicide than heterosexual youth.

○ More than half of adolescents who commit suicide have a history of alcohol or drug use.

○ Two studies document the role that the media can play in youth suicides. One indicated a significant increase in teen suicides the week after national news broadcasts about suicide, while another revealed a significant increase in attempted suicides by teens following the broadcast of three TV movies on suicide.

○ The risk of suicide is five times greater in homes in which there is a gun.

○ A gun is the most common method of teen suicide. Guns are used in approximately two thirds of suicides by individuals under eighteen.

Suicide Fictions

There are many misconceptions surrounding teen suicides. The following are some of the most common.

"PEOPLE COMMIT SUICIDE WITHOUT GIVING ANY WARNING." In fact, four out of five individuals who commit suicide give some warning of their intention, whether by making desperate comments or giving away prized possessions. The problem is that others may not pick up on these signs. We must be particularly attuned to the behavior and statements of emotionally fragile or socially isolated children.

"NOBODY WOULD KILL HERSELF OVER THAT." You may not understand how a teenager could take such a drastic step over what seems like an insubstantial reason. Bear in mind, however, that it is not how serious the problem seems to you but how seriously it is hurting the teen. Evaluate the severity of the problem from her perspective rather than your own. Try to remember what it was like to be a teenager—when a disappointment made you feel as though the world was coming to an end.

"IF A PERSON IS DETERMINED TO KILL HERSELF, NOTHING WILL STOP HER." Most people who attempt suicide are ambivalent, wavering between wanting to live and wanting to die. And many of those who attempt suicide want to end the pain more than they want to end their life. We must appeal to the part of the person that wants to live and provide her with hope that we can help relieve her pain.

"PEOPLE WHO TALK ABOUT SUICIDE WON'T REALLY DO IT." The reality is that the majority of those who attempt or commit suicide give some signs of their desperation, whether directly through statements of despair or indirectly through their behavior. The lesson here is that all suicide threats need to be taken seriously.

"PEOPLE WHO ATTEMPT OR COMMIT SUICIDE ARE MENTALLY ILL." While a teenager who tries to take her own life is no doubt emotionally distraught and perhaps even depressed, this does not mean that she is mentally ill or psychotic. Many teens who are suicidal have no psychiatric history, and their suicidal act may be an impulsive reaction to a major disappointment.

"TELLING AN ADULT ABOUT A FRIEND WHO IS THREATENING TO COMMIT SUICIDE IS BETRAYING HER TRUST." Teens who are suicidal may not see any way out of their pain other than taking their life. They may lack the energy and the sense of hope to seek help. Yet we know that teens who are depressed can be helped to feel more in control and more hopeful. Getting help for a suicidal peer by informing a guidance counselor, teacher, or parent is a courageous and compassionate act. Similarly, if your child tells you that a friend is threatening suicide, take this seriously and inform a school official or the friend's parents.

"TALKING ABOUT SUICIDE MAY PUT THE IDEA IN THE PERSON'S HEAD." If you fear that your child may be considering suicide, face the issue head-on. Ask her in a direct and open manner whether she has had thoughts of suicide. You will not be planting harmful ideas in her head; rather, you will be showing her that you take her distress seriously and are inviting her to talk about her feelings and share her pain. In addition, if she indicates in response to your question that she has been contemplating suicide, this will alert you to seek immediate help and monitor her behavior carefully.

"ONCE A TEENAGER IS FEELING BETTER AFTER AN EMOTIONAL CRISIS, SHE IS OUT OF DANGER." If your deeply distraught child shows signs of a more upbeat mood, this does not necessarily signal the resolution of the problem or the end of her despair. Rather, it may reflect the natural course of depression when a person may feel better on some days than others. If you sense that your child's mood is a bit more upbeat, this is not the time to lessen your vigilance. Suicides often occur when deeply depressed individuals experience a mild lifting of their mood and thus have the energy to act on their continuing despair.

"TEENAGERS DO NOT SUFFER FROM DEPRESSION." Nothing could be further from the truth. Depression can affect people of any age—and does.

"A TEENAGER THREATENING SUICIDE IS JUST TRYING TO GET ATTENTION OR MANIPULATE OTHERS." Those who have this misconception might conclude that we should give little attention to these threats, but experience tells us otherwise. People often talk about suicide before actually going ahead with the act. We cannot take the risk of ignoring children and teens who make these threats.

"TEENAGERS WHO ARE DEPRESSED NEED TO PULL THEMSELVES TOGETHER, AND NOBODY CAN DO THAT FOR THEM." Depression is not a character defect, nor does it reflect laziness or a lack of willpower. It is a serious problem that warrants professional help. And once teens get that help, whether through therapy, medication, or both, there is a good chance that their mental outlook will improve.

Teens and Depression

Depression is different from the "blues." While the blues are temporary feelings of sadness that many people experience, depression is a more long-term problem in which a person feels a pervasive sense of unhappiness and helplessness that can affect virtually every aspect of her life. The following list offers some important facts about depression.

- Depression is often misdiagnosed. It may be disguised as other problems such as an eating disorder, substance abuse, sexual promiscuity, or school phobia, or may involve attempts to run away from home.

- Depression can have many causes. Research points to a genetic link to some forms of depression so that it can sometimes run in families. Biology can also play a role: a deficiency or excess of brain chemicals called neurotransmitters can bring on depression. In addition, depression can be triggered by stressful life experiences in conjunction with certain personality characteristics, such as difficulty coping with stress or low self-esteem. In some cases depression can occur without any apparent cause or upsetting life event.

○ Depression can range from mild to severe and can assume various forms. Some individuals have bipolar depression in which their moods swing between two opposite extremes: depression, characterized by deep despair, and mania, characterized by frenzied activity and grandiose ideas.

○ Depressed teens have a higher rate of suicide than teens who are not depressed. The risk also increases if there is a family history of depression and suicide.

○ Teens may try to ease their emotional pain by using alcohol or drugs. This can increase their risk of suicide because it may deepen their depression, impair their judgment, and increase impulsiveness.

○ Depression is an equal-opportunity problem that can affect people of all ages (including children), races, ethnic groups, and socioeconomic backgrounds.

○ Depression is very treatable. It is estimated that 80 percent to 90 percent of individuals with depression can be helped through therapy, medication, or a combination of the two. Cognitive therapy, which focuses on changing a person's negative thoughts and inaccurate perceptions, has been particularly effective with depression.

○ Depressed teens often do not seek help because they do not recognize they are depressed or do not feel they can be helped.

○ Teens may be reluctant to talk with others about their struggles with depression. They may feel ashamed of their problem and fear that others may perceive them as weak, lazy, or even crazy. They may also assume that others will not care enough about their problems to help.

Is Your Child Depressed?

It is hard for parents to judge whether their child is depressed, especially if their teenage child is normally noncommunicative and moody, which is not uncommon for teens. The following list of signs of depression can help you determine if your child's sulky behavior goes beyond normal teen moodiness. Look for a pattern of behaviors that are ongoing rather than just using one behavior to conclude your child may be depressed.

PERSISTENT FEELINGS OF SADNESS. She may start crying without knowing why.

FEELINGS OF HOPELESSNESS AND WORTHLESSNESS. She may feel this way in spite of having a record of accomplishments.

GENERAL LACK OF ENERGY. She may appear as if she has slowed down.

LACK OF ENTHUSIASM FOR ACTIVITIES. Activities that previously brought her pleasure, such as talking on the phone, playing sports, or going to the mall, may now have little appeal to her.

WITHDRAWAL FROM FAMILY AND FRIENDS. She may spend most of her time alone and show little interest in getting together with friends.

DROP IN ACADEMIC MOTIVATION AND PERFORMANCE. She may start to cut classes and stay home from school. When in class, she may have difficulty concentrating.

CONFUSED THOUGHT PROCESS. She may have problems making decisions and remembering information.

SLOWED AND DISORGANIZED SPEECH. It may be hard to follow what she is saying.

INCREASED IRRITABILITY. She may get upset over small things that did not bother her before.

UNCONTROLLABLE OUTBURSTS OF ANGER. This may include aggressive acts toward others or self-injurious behavior.

INTENSE FEELINGS OF GUILT. She may blame herself for things that are not her fault.

THOUGHTS OF SUICIDE. She may talk openly and directly about wanting to end her life and may be preoccupied with themes of death.

SUBSTANCE ABUSE. She may use drugs or alcohol to "medicate" her pain and help her feel better.

VAGUE, NONSPECIFIC PHYSICAL COMPLAINTS. These may include stomachaches, headaches, low back pain, dizziness, or fatigue.

CHANGE IN SLEEPING PATTERNS. She may be sleeping too much or too little.

CHANGE OF APPETITE. This may result in significant weight gain or loss.

What to Say to a Depressed Teen

You may not be sure what to say to your depressed child, fearing that if you say the wrong thing it could make the situation worse. Do not try to fix the problem or minimize her concerns by saying such things as "This is just a stage. All kids go through it." Instead, reach out to her in a way that shows your concern. The following are examples of what you might say. Keep in mind that using the right words is less important than showing her that you care.

- "Help me understand what has been upsetting you."
- "I care about you. You are really important to me."
- "You mean a lot to me, and I don't want anything to happen to you."
- "I know you must really be in pain."
- "I can't imagine how much you must be hurting."
- "I will be there for you."
- "We will get through this together."

- "You may be feeling that things are hopeless, but I really believe that as time passes you will feel better."
- "I know some places we can call to get us some help."

Events That May Trigger a Suicide Attempt

Events or disappointments in a teen's life may turn her thoughts to suicide. Keep in mind that while some of the events may seem insignificant to you, they can be crushing to a teenager. Lacking a long-term perspective, she may perceive a temporary event as a permanent condition. Here are some possible events:

- The death or serious illness of a family member or close friend
- Divorce or separation
- Joining a new family with stepparents and stepsiblings
- Intense and ongoing conflict with parents
- Rejection by a family member
- Sexual abuse
- The move of a best friend
- Moving to a new community
- Peer rejection
- Frequent bullying from another student
- Breaking up with a boyfriend or girlfriend
- An embarrassing or humiliating episode witnessed by peers
- Rites of passage such as graduation or transition times such as a return to school
- Significant academic problems such as a dramatic drop in grades
- A harsh reprimand or disciplinary action by an important adult figure such as a parent or teacher

- An unwanted pregnancy
- A serious problem with the law
- The suicide of one or more fellow students (this phenomenon is called a suicide cluster)
- Viewing stories of suicide in the media

Warning Signs That Your Child May Be Considering Suicide

Teens who are depressed often try to hide their feelings, but the majority of those who attempt suicide give some warning signs of their intentions. Keep in mind that a teen who displays one or even a few of these signs is not necessarily suicidal, but it does suggest a need for some professional help. The following behaviors may be seen in a depressed teen who is considering suicide.

- Previous suicidal attempt
- Making statements indicating suicidal intentions (such as "I'm really hurting, and I want to end the pain" or "Nothing matters anymore")
- Statements of hopelessness
- Writing essays or poems or doing artwork that has death themes
- Putting her affairs in order (such as giving away her favorite possessions or cleaning her room)
- Dramatic personality changes (for example, angry or agitated behavior)
- Engaging in risky or reckless behavior (for example, driving fast or walking across a busy street carelessly)
- Loss of interest in activities that she previously enjoyed
- Withdrawal from family and friends

- Calling or visiting individuals she cares about to say good-bye
- Problems in dealing with or accepting her sexual orientation
- Declining interest in academic performance
- Unusual neglect of her physical appearance
- Self-inflicted injuries such as cuts, scratches, or burns
- Significant change in sleeping or eating habits
- Increasing use of alcohol or drugs
- Frequent complaints of physical discomfort such as stomachaches or headaches

Helping Your Depressed or Suicidal Child

While you need to obtain professional help for your child if she appears depressed or suicidal, you also play a critical role in providing her with support. You can take the following steps to help your child:

DO NOT PANIC. Bear in mind that a teen considering suicide can usually be helped through a combination of professional treatment and understanding and support from friends and family.

TAKE HER CONCERNS SERIOUSLY. A threat of suicide is a desperate cry for help. Respond to a threat with the utmost seriousness. Do not under any circumstances ignore or trivialize the threat because this will intensify her desperation.

LISTEN TO YOUR CHILD. Encourage her to speak about what is upsetting her. Let her unburden herself.

RESPOND IN A CARING, COMPASSIONATE MANNER. Give her comfort rather than advice, caring instead of criticism. Provide a safe haven of love and understanding. Help her feel understood rather than blamed. Avoid arguments with her at all costs.

DO NOT MINIMIZE HER PROBLEMS. Acknowledge your child's feelings and perceptions even if they seem trivial to you. If she perceives a problem as serious, then it is serious to her.

AVOID GIVING ADVICE OR TRYING TO MAKE HER FEEL BETTER. Giving her advice or trying to talk her out of being depressed by telling her how good she has it will only intensify her feelings of guilt and hopelessness. Instead, listen attentively to her concerns and help her feel that she has been understood.

GIVE YOUR CHILD A SENSE OF HOPE. Many teens who are depressed or contemplating suicide have abandoned hope. They may have little faith that anyone can relieve their pain. Reassure your child that others who have gone through a similar experience have been helped to feel better. Explain that what she is feeling is temporary and with time and help her pain will ease. Let her know that you will be by her side throughout the ordeal.

ASK HER IF SHE HAS THOUGHT OF SUICIDE. If you fear that she may be contemplating suicide, do not sidestep the issue. Ask her directly and openly if she has been thinking about it. Bringing this up will convey your concern, let her know that you are taking her problems seriously, and open the lines of communication.

IF SHE IS THINKING OF SUICIDE, ASK FURTHER QUESTIONS. The purpose is to gauge how serious she is about suicide and whether she is in immediate danger. Ask her in a calm manner if she has a plan to kill herself and whether she has taken any steps toward carrying it out (for example, obtaining a gun). If she has formulated a plan and has access to the means, consider the risk of suicide high. If so, obtain professional help immediately.

DO NOT LEAVE YOUR CHILD ALONE IF YOU FEAR SHE MAY TRY TO HARM HERSELF. If necessary, take her to a crisis center or the emergency room of a hospital.

GET HELP FOR YOUR CHILD. She may feel that her situation is hopeless and that no one can help her. Let her know that most teenagers with problems like hers have been helped by professionals. Explain that the professional will not be looking to find fault with her but rather to help her feel better.

SUICIDE-PROOF YOUR HOUSE. Keep in mind that the risk of suicide is five times greater in homes in which there is a gun. For those intent on committing suicide, a gun represents a quick and sure method. If you have a gun in your home and your child is showing signs of being depressed or suicidal, make sure it is unloaded and inaccessible to her. Better yet, remove it from your home. Also consider removing other potentially dangerous items such as medications, knives, razors, and ropes.

INFORM THE SCHOOL. Meet with key people at your child's school such as her teachers, guidance counselor, and school psychologist to inform them of her emotional difficulties so they can monitor her, ease any stressful situations, and let you know if concerns surface. Tell them that you expect this information to be kept confidential.

GET HELP FOR YOURSELF. Just as your child may need help, you also may need help if she is going through an emotional crisis. It may be difficult for you to accept or understand her problems, and you may feel partially to blame. You may need help sorting through these feelings as well as learning how best to respond to your child. Your family may also need support and guidance in dealing with difficulties such as parental conflict, poor communication, or parental substance abuse that may be contributing to your child's depression. Help may take various forms: individual counseling, family counseling, or a support group for parents of troubled teens.

Finding Help for Your Child

With family and professional support, a child who is feeling depressed or suicidal can be helped. Do not resist getting help for your child on the assumption that the problem will simply go away. While feelings of sadness and despair can fade with time, they can also build to the point where the teen feels that suicide is her only option. The following are sources of help for your child:

⚬ Psychiatrist (a medical doctor who is authorized to prescribe medication)

- Psychologist

- Social worker

- Pastoral counselor

- Community mental health center

- Family services agency

- Depression or mood disorders clinic

- Crisis center

- Department of psychiatry at local hospital

- Hospital emergency room

- Suicide hotline

You may be able to get a recommendation for professional help from your child's pediatrician, the school psychologist, the school social worker, friends, or family members. Be sure to find someone who is experienced in working with adolescents. Check the yellow pages for the phone numbers of a local suicide hotline, crisis centers, and mental health agencies.

Your child may resist seeing a counselor. She may fear that the counselor will lecture her about her personal failings and only intensify her pain and distress. Reassure her that therapy will be a support to her, not a burden. Consider whether your child may benefit from group support. She may find it helpful to meet and talk with peers who are going through similar problems.

You may be reluctant to seek help for yourself and your child for fear that you will be blamed for her problems. This is unlikely. What is more likely is that the counselor will be looking to support and guide you rather than find fault with you. Don't let this fear delay your getting help for your child. In deciding on a counselor, consider whether your child will respond better to a male or a female. If money is an issue, find out if the local mental health center has a sliding scale.

As part of the treatment it may be suggested that your child obtain a physical examination to determine if there is a physical basis for her depression.

Helping Your Child Readjust After a Suicide Attempt

Helping your child cope after a suicide attempt presents serious challenges. Consider the following steps to ease her adjustment.

Continue with Professional Help. Do not assume that whatever was upsetting your child will simply fade away.

Be Available to Your Child. Make sure she knows how to contact you during the day. If she does ask for your help, try to give her immediate attention.

Avoid Grilling Her About Her Suicide Attempt. This will likely upset her and make her feel abnormal.

Monitor Her Behavior Without Being Intrusive. While you will understandably be much more attentive to her behavior after a suicide attempt, you will need to avoid constantly intruding on her privacy. You will need to find a balance between being attentive and being intrusive. The latter is likely to cause a backlash.

Help Your Child Get Back into a Routine. Encourage her to resume her normal activities and get back on track in school. At the same time, do not rush her back into the activities that were causing her stress.

Help Her Figure Out What to Say to Peers. Your child will need some guidance in knowing how to answer the inevitable questions she will face from classmates. Give her suggestions of what to say and, if she is willing, role-play with her.

Keep Dangerous Items Out of the House. Bear in mind that there is a risk of another suicide attempt.

CONSULT WITH YOUR CHILD'S SCHOOL. It is important that key people in school—the principal, her guidance counselor, the school psychologist, and teachers—be alerted to her emotional crisis. Make it clear that this information is to be kept confidential. Talk with the school staff about how to make up missed work and also lessen some of the stress she may be feeling in school.

AFTER THE SUICIDE OF A SIBLING OR FRIEND, A CHILD MAY FEEL . . .

. . . *sad* at the loss of her sibling or friend.

. . . *angry* at the person who took her life and at others as well.

. . . *scared* that she, too, might die.

. . . *embarrassed* to return to school and have to face awkward questions from peers.

. . . *confused* about why her sibling or friend took her life.

. . . *abandoned* by her sibling or friend and filled with a sense of loneliness.

. . . *guilty* that she might have done more to keep her sibling or friend from taking her life.

. . . *at fault* for saying or doing something that she fears drove her sibling or friend to suicide.

. . . *afraid* that someone else she cares about will also take her life.

. . . *nothing at all.* She may go into a state of denial and pretend that nothing happened.

A child who has experienced the loss of a sibling or friend may ride an emotional roller coaster in the aftermath of the suicide. She will likely need support from family and perhaps professional counseling to come to grips with and make sense of her loss and her emotions.

Factors That Make Suicide Less Likely

Teens can react very differently to life crises. Where one teen may demonstrate resilience and good coping skills, another may feel a sense of utter hopelessness to the point of contemplating suicide. The following factors may give a teen the emotional resolve to confront problems without letting them overwhelm her:

A Supportive and Caring Family. A caring and understanding family is an important source of support for any teen, especially a troubled one. This means you should make it a priority to maintain a strong and trusting relationship with your child, spend quality time with her, build and maintain good communication with her, and make certain to convey that her views are listened to and understood. In addition, it is important for her to feel that you respect her privacy.

A Stable and Secure Home Environment. Children who experience significant family changes, whether separation, divorce, death, or financial stress, may learn the hard way about the fragility of life. This stress is magnified when these family changes are not handled with a concern for the child's welfare (for example, a child becoming a pawn in a parental dispute).

Support During Times of Stress. When teens face what they perceive to be traumatic events, such as peer rejection, bullying, family breakup, or academic difficulties, to name only a few, they need to know there is someone they can count on for support and understanding. Your child may look to you as a lifeline, but she may also seek another adult, such as a relative, teacher, coach, or close friend. Teens who lack this support may fall victim to despair, and their thoughts may turn to suicide.

A Supportive Peer Network. As children enter their teen years, peer support may become even more important than family support. During times of emotional crisis a teen may first look to friends for guidance and understanding. Teens who lack a sense of belonging and support from their peers may feel they have no one to turn to during such times.

GOOD COPING SKILLS. Teens who are resourceful, resilient, and skilled in problem solving are better able to cope with stressful situations. A child with good coping skills may react to a stressful situation with determination rather than despair. When a child with limited personal resources faces stressful events that exceed her ability to cope, she may experience suicidal thoughts.

INVOLVEMENT IN COMMUNITY ACTIVITIES. Teens can gain a sense of belonging and self-esteem from school or community activities. These activities may also offer them an opportunity to channel their emotions and frustration in a socially acceptable manner. Try to find activities for your child with peers she can relate to, with an opportunity for her to enjoy success, and with supervision provided by caring and responsible adults.

EARLY DETECTION OF EMOTIONAL PROBLEMS. Serious emotional problems such as schizophrenia, bipolar depression, and anorexia, which can emerge during adolescence, carry a higher risk of suicide. Detecting these problems early and providing appropriate help can lessen the chance that the individual will contemplate suicide.

RECOMMENDED READING

Books for Teens

Cobain, B. (1998). *When Nothing Matters Anymore: A Survival Guide for Depressed Teens.* Minneapolis, MN: Free Spirit Publishing (grades 8 and up).

Crook, M. (1997). *Suicide: Teens Talk to Teens.* Bellingham, WA: Self-Counsel Press.

Irwin, C. (1999). *Conquering the Beast Within: How I Fought Depression and Won and How You Can, Too.* New York: Crown Publishing Group (written by a teenager about her experience with depression).

Books for Parents

Dubuque, S. E. (1996). *A Parent's Survival Guide to Childhood Depression.* King of Prussia, PA: Center for Applied Psychology.

Frankel, B., and Kranz, R. (1994). *Straight Talk About Teenage Suicide.* New York: Facts on File.

Jamison, K. R. (1999). *Night Falls Fast: Understanding Suicide.* New York: Alfred A. Knopf.

Shamoo, T., and Patros, P. G. (1996). *Helping Your Child Cope with Depression and Suicidal Thoughts.* San Francisco: Jossey-Bass.

Slaby, A. E., and Garfinkel, L. F. (1996). *No One Saw My Pain: Why Teens Kill Themselves.* New York: Norton.

Williams, K. (1995). *A Parent's Guide for Suicidal and Depressed Teens: Help for Recognizing if a Child Is in Crisis and What to Do About It.* Center City, MN: Hazelden.

ORGANIZATIONS

American Association of Suicidology

4201 Connecticut Avenue, NW, Suite 408
Washington, DC 20008
1-202-237-2280
www.suicidology.org

Dedicated to the understanding and prevention of suicide. Offers resources for suicide prevention and referrals for those who have lost a loved one to suicide.

The Compassionate Friends

P. O. Box 3696
Oak Brook, IL 60522
1-877-969-0010
www.compassionatefriends.org

A national self-help organization that provides support to parents following the death of their child and information to help others be supportive.

National Depressive and Manic-Depressive Association

730 North Franklin Street, Suite 501
Chicago, IL 60610-7204
1-800-826-3632
www.ndmda.org

Educates parents, families, professionals, and the public about depression and manic depression, and promotes self-help for patients and families.

National Suicide Hotline

1-800-SUICIDE (784-2433)

SA\VE—Suicide Awareness\Voices of Education

7317 Cahill Road, Suite 207
Minneapolis, MN 55439
1-952-946-7998
www.save.org

Educates the public about suicide and depression.

CHAPTER 10

Promoting Healthy Media Habits

The impact of media violence is no longer open to debate. Over one thousand studies over many decades have confirmed what many parents have long feared: media violence encourages violent behavior. Children, who are easily swayed by what they see and hear, are particularly vulnerable to media violence. They learn how to behave, how to deal with people, and how to cope with problems partly by what they see in the media. Even children as young as fourteen months have been observed to repeat behavior they have seen on television.

The problem of media violence is particularly alarming when you consider the prominent place that media play in the lives of our children. While television continues to be the single most important media influence on children, it now competes with movies, video games, computer games, music, and even comic books in shaping their values and behavior. Children are exposed to a steady diet of media—and much of it is violent. By the age of eighteen a typical child will have seen about sixteen thousand murders and have viewed over two hundred thousand acts of violence on television.

Consider the following media sampling to which your child may be exposed:

- A video game where a player can make a monster follow and threaten frightened, scantily clad young women

- A computer game in which a mailman goes around town shooting people, with bonus points awarded if a player shoots a person in the head, execution-style

- Movies with intense and graphic violence that children can watch at home but would not be allowed to watch in movie theaters

- Violent video games with such names as *Killer Instinct*, *Street Fighter*, and *Lethal Enforcer*

- Lyrics to a popular song that ask: "Who says date rape isn't kind?"

- An advertisement for a video game that reads: "Let the slaughter begin."

- A video game called *Turok 2: Seeds of Evil*, in which a player can use a "cerebral bore" to rip a character's head open

- Animated and live-action television shows in which characters are badly hurt in one show, but return to the next show without any sign of injury or discomfort from the violence

- Video games such as *Duck Hunt* and *Time Crisis* that are virtually identical to training devices used by the military

The message that children learn from these and countless other sources of media violence is loud and clear: violence is common and acceptable.

There has always been violence on television and in the movies, but the violence children witness today is decidedly different. It is more graphic, more intense, more realistic, and more frightening. Unfortunately, for many children and teens it is also more exciting. And yet as intense as the violence sometimes is, viewers are often shielded from its consequences. The camera may quickly cut away from a scene so there is no evidence of injury or death. It is violence without pain, or what one commentator called "happy violence."

While media violence is certainly not the only cause of violence in our society, it unquestionably plays a large role. Fortunately, we can do something about it. The entertainment industry and the government can use their influence and power to rein in media violence, but there is no substitute for close parental monitoring. Parents must assume primary responsibility for lessening their children's exposure to media violence and helping them put into perspective the violence they will see.

A Few Facts About Children's Media Habits

- The typical American home has three televisions, three cassette players, three radios, two VCRs, two CD players, a video game player, and a computer.

- About 65 percent of American children have a TV in their room.

- The television is on for about seven hours a day in a typical American household.

- American children watch an average of three to four hours of television a day. They spend more time watching television each week than any activity other than sleeping.

- Children spend an average of 4.8 hours per day or 33.6 hours per week using the television, VCR, computer, and video games.

- By the time a child graduates from high school he will most likely have watched about 15,000 hours of television and listened to 10,500 hours of popular music—compared with 13,000 hours spent in school.

- A child will see an average of twenty thousand TV commercials every year.

- Supervision of children's television viewing is often lacking. About 50 percent of children do not have any parental restrictions on the amount of time they spend watching television or the programs they watch.

What Research Tells Us About
Media Violence

- Fifty-seven percent of television programs contain some violence.

- Children's television programs, including cartoons, contain more violence than any other form of programming. There are three to five violent incidents per hour in prime time compared with twenty to twenty-five per hour on children's programming on Saturday morning. The average cartoon has twenty-six violent incidents.

- Ninety-four percent of video games have violent content.

- When asked in a 1993 survey what kinds of video games they preferred, 32 percent of children chose "fantasy violence," 17 percent chose "human violence," and only 2 percent chose "educational games."

- MTV music videos include an average of twenty-nine acts of violence per hour, ranging from vandalism to vicious brawls to sexual violence against women.

- During the past forty years more than one thousand studies have been conducted on the impact of media violence. The majority of these studies indicate that television and film violence contributes to aggressive behavior in children.

- Children who watch television or play video games for more than two hours a day are more likely to exhibit impulsive behaviors and less likely to persist when faced with challenging mental problems.

- More than half of the violent incidents seen on television or in the movies would be fatal or physically debilitating if they were to happen in real life.

- In 1998 only 21 percent of retail and rental stores had any policies prohibiting the sale or rental of adult games to minors.

⊙ Children are less likely to be negatively affected by media violence, advertising, and stereotyped portrayals when parents discuss with them what they have seen.

How Does Media Violence Affect Children?

Media violence leaves its imprint on children of all ages, intellectual abilities, and socioeconomic levels. Of course, not every child who is exposed to violence on television or in video games will grow up to be violent; most leave their aggression on the screen. But the more media violence your child is exposed to, the more he is likely to:

⊙ view aggression as an acceptable way of solving problems.

⊙ be aggressive and "bullying" in dealing with others.

⊙ be insensitive to the pain and suffering of victims of violence.

⊙ be less capable of responding to those who are hurting.

⊙ overestimate the likelihood that he will become a victim of violence.

⊙ be preoccupied with protecting himself.

⊙ be fearful of being alone.

⊙ be mistrustful of people in general.

⊙ experience anxiety and have nightmares.

⊙ perceive the world as a mean and dangerous place.

⊙ have poor peer relationships.

⊙ be rated poorly by his teachers.

⊙ have problems learning and concentrating in school.

⊙ have problems with the law as a teenager.

⊙ have an increased desire for viewing violence in the media as well as in real life.

- perceive that there are few consequences to committing violent acts.

- believe that violence is the way society typically handles conflict.

How to Promote Healthy Media Habits

Research tells us that the television viewing habits of young children often affect their television habits as adults, so help your child develop healthy television (and other media) practices at an early age by doing the following:

ESTABLISH TELEVISION-VIEWING GUIDELINES. Consider keeping a log of your child's viewing patterns for one week. Once you have an idea of how much TV he watches, you can develop some realistic rules. These rules may restrict the number of hours, the times of the day, and the programs your child can watch. Consider his age in developing these guidelines. You may also want to set some limits on his use of video and computer games. (The next section offers some sample media guidelines.)

COORDINATE WITH OTHER PARENTS ABOUT TELEVISION GUIDELINES. The pressure your child feels to watch certain programs might be lessened if his friends have similar restrictions.

DESIGNATE CERTAIN TIMES OF THE DAY WHEN THE TELEVISION IS TURNED OFF. This might be during meals, homework, or family quiet time. If you have a VCR, record your child's favorite shows for viewing at another time.

GIVE THOUGHT TO WHERE YOU PLACE THE TV. You might decrease your child's television time by placing the TV in an area that allows you to easily monitor his viewing. Avoid having the television become the focal point of your home.

KEEP A TV AND VCR OUT OF YOUR CHILD'S BEDROOM. He is likely to watch more television if he has a TV in his room. Keeping it out of his room is the only way you will be able to exercise some reasonable control over his television viewing.

DO NOT USE THE TELEVISION OR VIDEO GAMES AS A BABY-SITTER. It may be tempting, especially when you're busy, to allow your child to sit in front of the TV for long stretches, but it can result in his using TV or video games as his main source of entertainment.

SUGGEST ALTERNATIVE ACTIVITIES. It may be easier for your child to turn on the TV than to figure out what else to do. Help him by suggesting or planning some attractive alternatives.

SET A GOOD EXAMPLE FOR YOUR CHILD. Children often adopt the television habits of their parents. Teach your child to be a discriminating viewer by being discriminating yourself. Watch programs consistent with the values you promote to your child.

TEACH YOUR CHILD TO BE A WISE VIEWER. Help him become selective in what he watches by having him go through the television listings at the beginning of the week or in the early evening to choose the shows he wants to watch that fit within the time constraints you have set. Discourage him from "channel surfing."

WATCH TELEVISION WITH YOUR CHILD, LISTEN TO HIS FAVORITE MUSIC, AND TRY SOME OF HIS VIDEO GAMES. This enables you to monitor his media exposure. Try to watch at least one episode of each of his favorite television shows. Talk with him about the programs to find out the impact the program has on him. For example, ask "What do you like about the program?" Also talk with him about negative images or faulty impressions contained in the programs.

ENCOURAGE YOUR CHILD TO WATCH PROGRAMS WITH MINIMAL VIOLENCE, WITH CHARACTERS WHO CARE FOR EACH OTHER, AND WITH FAIR PORTRAYALS OF PEOPLE. You might assign a point value to programs and then allow your child to watch shows totaling a set number of points over the course of a week. Less desirable programs can be assigned a higher point value.

EDUCATE YOUR CHILD ABOUT ADVERTISEMENTS. Children, especially preschoolers, may not understand that the purpose of commercials is to sell products. Indeed, they may not know the difference between a commercial and a program. Help your child understand this purpose and let him know that a commercial will sometimes exaggerate or mislead viewers. You may also want to give him a lesson in nutrition to counter enticing ads for unhealthy foods.

AVOID BUYING YOUR CHILD A VIDEO GAME SYSTEM AS LONG AS POSSIBLE. He is less likely to get hooked on these games if he starts at a later age. In addition, it may be easier for you to restrict his video time and game choices at a later age.

ENCOURAGE YOUR CHILD'S SCHOOL TO TEACH MEDIA LITERACY. In this way he can learn to think critically about what he sees and hears in the media, to appreciate the impact of media violence, and to understand the role of media advertising. Children who are media savvy are more resistant to harmful media effects.

Sample Media Guidelines for Your Home

You may want to consider the following media rules for your child. Decide which ones work for you, taking into consideration your own values as well as your child's age.

- Allow your child to watch no more than two hours of television in a single day (a recommendation of the American Academy of Pediatrics) and no more than a total of ten hours a week (a Federal Commission on Reading recommendation).

- Limit your child to one hour of television on school nights and two hours on other nights.

- Do not let your child watch television or play video games before school.

- Do not allow your child to watch television while he does homework.

- Prohibit television or video games until your child's homework is done.

- Turn the television off during meals.

- Prohibit television viewing and video game playing on school nights.

- Make a rule that for every hour spent watching television or playing video or computer games, your child must spend comparable time involved in a constructive activity such as reading, doing homework, working on an art project, or practicing an instrument.

- Establish a family quiet time during the evening when the television is turned off.

- Set aside one night a week when the television is off-limits to family members (including parents) and engage in some activity that all of you enjoy.

- Consider having a television-free weekend or week in your home periodically. Make up a list with your child of activities he would like to do during that time and see how many you can accomplish.

- Use a timer to limit the amount of time your child plays video or computer games.

Using TV to Enhance Your Child's Knowledge and Skills

You can help make television a productive and educational activity by doing the following:

- Tape shows that relate to your child's interests or hobbies.

- Look for television programs that relate to topics being covered in your child's class. Ask the teacher what science or social studies topics he will be studying.

- Ask the teacher or school librarian for her recommendations of videos relating to school topics.

- Find programs for your child to watch that mirror real life more accurately and that are slower paced than the typically fast-paced programs that children watch.

- Promote critical thinking by talking with your child about the program and asking questions such as "What do you think will happen next?" "Why do you think he did that?" or "How do you think she felt?"

- Ask your child to tell you the story of a program he has watched.

- Encourage your child to read books or magazines based on television programs he has liked. A program related to a historical figure may spur him to read a biography of the person.

- Suggest that your child do an art project related to a television program he has seen (for example, a collage or puppet based on a character in a show).

- Encourage your older child to watch the news and point out stories that relate to what he is studying in school.

Reducing Your Child's Exposure to Media Violence

While you may be able to lessen your child's exposure to media violence, you will not be able to eliminate it entirely. After all, you have limited control over what he does or watches when a babysitter is caring for him, when he is over a friend's house, or when you are not home. You can, however, help lessen the impact of media violence on your child by taking these steps:

MAKE SOME VIOLENT OR OFFENSIVE PROGRAMS OFF LIMITS. In deciding what to prohibit, keep in mind your child's age and maturity level. As a general rule, avoid realistic violent scenes if your child is under the age of nine. You may not want to prohibit all programs or movies with violence. Indeed, some violent scenes in movies or TV programs are appropriate, convey a respect for life, and foster sensitivity and empathy.

USE A RATING SYSTEM TO EVALUATE A PROGRAM, MOVIE, OR GAME. The following two rating systems use parents, teachers, and children to assess the suitability of television programs, movies, and video games:

- *KidScore.* This rating system is sponsored by the National Institute on Media and Family, and can be found online at www.mediafamily.org/kidscore.

- *Kids First.* This rating system is sponsored by the Coalition for Quality Children's Media, and can be found online at www.cqcm.org/kidsfirst.

HELP YOUR CHILD DISTINGUISH BETWEEN REAL AND PRETEND. Young children often believe that characters on shows actually exist, that the events are real, and that victims of violence are really hurt.

TALK WITH YOUR CHILD ABOUT THE PROGRAMS HE HAS WATCHED. In this way you can inoculate your child against the values on TV that are counter to yours. Let him know how you feel about the violent incidents. Explain that there are other ways to solve a problem and solicit your child's ideas about how the character might have handled the situation without using violence. Possible questions to ask your child when discussing a program are in the following section.

BE ESPECIALLY CAREFUL ABOUT WHAT YOUR CHILD WATCHES JUST BEFORE BEDTIME. Violent or scary images may stick with him and keep him from getting to sleep.

MONITOR YOUR CHILD'S REACTIONS TO SCARY OR VIOLENT PROGRAMS. Your child may convey fear or distress by clinging to you, crying, covering his eyes, or running from the room. Long-term reactions may show up in the form of sleeping problems, nightmares, reluctance to sleep alone, changes in eating patterns, clingy behavior, or avoidance of certain places or activities.

COMFORT YOUR CHILD IF HE IS FEARFUL. If a young child is upset by a frightening or violent program, turn it off or remove him from the area and divert his attention by having him engage in a pleasant activity. If necessary, sit with him and give him physical comfort. You might have him draw a picture of what scared him; this will help him gain a sense of control. You may find that talking with him can ease his fears.

BUY A TELEVISION WITH A V-CHIP. This computer chip allows parents to block shows that contain violence, sex, language, and other material they deem unsuitable for their children.

LOCK OUT CHANNELS YOU DON'T WANT YOUR CHILD TO SEE. Your cable company may offer this option that you can access with a key or a remote control requiring a personal identification number.

COMMUNICATE YOUR MEDIA RESTRICTIONS TO CARETAKERS. Ask for the cooperation of neighbors, grandparents, babysitters, and others who care for your child to limit his viewing of violence.

MONITOR YOUR CHILD'S VIDEO AND VIDEO GAME RENTALS OR PURCHASES. Bear in mind that you retain veto power over videos and video and computer games. You should offer your child an explanation for those you reject.

GET HELP FOR A CHILD OBSESSED WITH WATCHING VIOLENT PROGRAMS. If your child has a significant appetite for watching violent programs or playing violent games and is acting aggressively with peers, taking steps to restrict his exposure to media violence may not be adequate. Consider seeking help from a counselor or psychologist.

Questions to Stimulate Your Child's Thinking About TV

As vigilant as you may be, you will not be able to supervise your child every time he watches TV or plays a video game. You can, however, help him understand the real-life consequences of what he sees by asking him questions about the programs he watches. These discussions will help him resist the influences of media violence, stereotypes, and commercialism. The following are examples of questions you might ask your child to stimulate his thinking:

- What did you like or dislike about the program?

- What was your favorite part of the program?

- Which character did you like best?

- Do you think the story would have happened that way in real life?

- What was the problem the character was facing? How did he try to solve it?

- Do you think that was the right way to deal with the situation?

- How else might the character have solved the problem without being violent?

- What would you have done if you were in his situation?

- Was the violence in the show realistic? Was anything left out?

- If a person actually did that in real life, what do you think would have happened to him?

- What would have happened to the victims of violence in real life? Could they have died or suffered permanent injury?

- How do you think the victim of the violence felt?
- How else might the show have ended?
- What did you learn from this program?
- Would you tell your friends to watch this program? Why or why not?

YOUR CHILD MAY BE SPENDING TOO MUCH TIME PLAYING VIDEO AND COMPUTER GAMES IF HE . . .

. . . plays them on an almost daily basis.

. . . plays them for many hours at a time.

. . . is spending most of his free time playing these games.

. . . is misleading you about the time he spends playing them.

. . . shows little interest in other activities because he is so involved with these games.

. . . prefers video games to playing with friends.

. . . plays them when he should be doing homework.

. . . gets very excited when playing so that he is seemingly oblivious to anything else going on around him.

. . . becomes very frustrated if he cannot play them.

. . . becomes angry and resists your efforts to limit his playing time.

Doing Your Share to Decrease Media Violence

Your voice, when combined with those of many other parents, can exert a powerful influence on the entertainment industry. Here are some actions you can take to curb violence in the media:

PROMOTE DISCUSSION OF THESE ISSUES. You may want to lead a discussion on media violence at a PTA meeting or in your church or synagogue.

JOIN AN ORGANIZATION WORKING TO REDUCE MEDIA VIOLENCE. To get started, see *Organizations* on page 221.

LOBBY THE ENTERTAINMENT INDUSTRY. Contact people involved in producing various media—television network and cable executives, producers and directors, television and movie writers, video game manufacturers, musicians and music producers—and urge them to decrease the violent content in their work. Encourage them to label their programs with parental advisory warnings and schedule those with content unsuitable to children for showing late at night. Press them to portray the consequences that violence can have on people and families.

GET IN TOUCH WITH SPONSORS OF VIOLENT PROGRAMS. Companies are very responsive to bottom-line concerns. Let sponsors of violent programs know that you will stop purchasing their products or services and will encourage others to do the same until they discontinue sponsoring such programs. Also inform them that research indicates violent shows hinder a viewer's memory of commercials, so it may be more cost effective for them to sponsor nonviolent programs. (This research can be found at www.apa.org/journals/xap/xap44291.html.)

VISIT YOUR LOCAL TELEVISION STATION. Ask how it is fulfilling its federal mandate to provide children with educational and informational programming. Also inquire what it is doing to decrease children's exposure to violence in its programming.

ENCOURAGE THE MEDIA TO PARTICIPATE IN A ONE-DAY MORATORIUM ON MEDIA VIOLENCE. This is typically held each October during national Child Health Month.

Movie Ratings Guidelines

The following list defines the ratings that movies receive from the Motion Picture Association of America's Rating Board. These are broad guidelines, of course, and what the rating board deems appropriate for your child may not meet your standards. Ultimately, the only expert on what your child should and should not see is you.

G: GENERAL AUDIENCES. ALL AGES ADMITTED. The movie does not contain material that parents are likely to find offensive. The rating does not suggest, however, that this is necessarily a movie of interest to children.

PG: PARENTAL GUIDANCE SUGGESTED. SOME MATERIAL MAY NOT BE SUITABLE FOR CHILDREN. Parents should consider reviewing the film due to the possibility of strong language, violence, or sexual content.

PG-13: PARENTS STRONGLY CAUTIONED. SOME MATERIAL MAY BE INAPPROPRIATE FOR CHILDREN UNDER THIRTEEN. The film rated may contain scenes with harsh language, violence, nudity, sexual content, and drug use.

R: RESTRICTED. UNDER SEVENTEEN REQUIRES ACCOMPANYING PARENT OR ADULT GUARDIAN. The film is likely to include one or more of the following elements: offensive language, violence, nudity, sexual scenes, or drug use.

NC-17: NO ONE SEVENTEEN AND UNDER ADMITTED. The movie is deemed inappropriate for individuals seventeen and under, and theater owners are barred from permitting persons of this age to view the film.

Using Television Ratings

The television industry has established a voluntary rating system consisting of both age-based and content-based designations.

Programs are assigned to various categories based on the degree to which they contain profanity or offensive language, violence, or sexual scenes. These labels are intended to be used with the "V-chip" device (which allows parents to block shows with specific ratings) and are briefly displayed on the television screen prior to the showing of a rated program.

AGE-BASED DESIGNATIONS

TV-Y: ALL CHILDREN. These programs are intended for young children and lack frightening content.

TV-Y7: DIRECTED TO CHILDREN AGES SEVEN AND ABOVE. These programs are suitable for children who can distinguish between fantasy and reality. They may include some mild fantasy and violence, and may frighten younger children.

TV-G: GENERAL AUDIENCE. These programs contain little or no violence, harsh language, or sexually suggestive dialogue. They are deemed appropriate for children of all ages.

TV-PG: PARENTAL GUIDANCE SUGGESTED. Parents may want to be familiar with the programs before allowing their child to view them because they may be inappropriate for younger children.

TV-14: PARENTS STRONGLY CAUTIONED. Because of the content of these programs, parents are advised not to allow children under the age of fourteen to watch them or to let them watch only with an adult present.

TV-MA: MATURE AUDIENCES ONLY. These are intended for viewing by adults and thus may be inappropriate for children under seventeen. They may contain violence, sexual scenes, or offensive language.

CONTENT-BASED DESIGNATIONS

The following content rating is used with programs labeled "TV-Y7":

FV: FANTASY VIOLENCE. This label is given to programs where the fantasy violence is particularly intense.

The following content ratings are used with programs labeled "TV-PG," "TV-14," and "TV-MA":

V: Violence

S: Sexual Situations

L: Coarse Language

D: Suggestive Dialogue

The Music Rating System

The Recording Industry Association of America (RIAA) has developed a "Parental Advisory" label that can assist parents in identifying music that may not be appropriate for children. The Parental Advisory logo is applied to the outside packaging of recordings that contain strong language or depictions of violence, sex, or substance abuse. Although the decision to label a particular recording is up to the record company that produces it, the RIAA indicates that "virtually every recording which has generated controversy in the media carries the Parental Advisory label." Many stores support this program by refusing to sell CDs that carry the Parental Advisory label to those under eighteen years of age.

RECOMMENDED READING

Canter, L., and Canter, M. (1996). *Couch Potato Kids: Teaching Kids to Turn Off the TV and Tune In to Fun.* Santa Monica, CA: Lee Canter & Associates.

Cantor, J. (1998). *Mommy, I'm Scared: How TV and Movies Frighten Children and What We Can Do to Protect Them.* San Diego: Harcourt.

DeGaetano, G. M. (1994). *Television and the Lives of Our Children: A Manual for Teachers and Parents.* Redmond, WA: Train of Thought Publishing.

Grossman, D., and DeGaetano, G. (1999). *Stop Teaching Our Kids to Kill: A Call to Action Against TV, Movie, and Video Game Violence.* New York: Crown Publishers.

New York Times. (1999). *The New York Times Guide to the Best Children's Videos.* New York: Pocket Books.

ORGANIZATIONS

LimiTV

P. O. Box 52122

Raleigh, NC 27612

1-888-546-4883

www.limitv.org

Seeks to inform parents, educators, and children about the ways excessive television watching can harm a child's development and education. It also sponsors an organization called The North Carolina Coalition for Pulling the Plug on Media Violence, which can be accessed through LimiTV's website.

National Alliance for Non-Violent Programming

122 North Elm Street, Suite 300

Greensboro, NC 27401

1-336-370-0407

A network of organizations committed to promoting nonviolence by reducing the impact of media violence through community action, advocacy, and education.

National Institute on Media and the Family

606 24th Avenue South, Suite 606

Minneapolis, MN 55454

1-888-672-5437

www.mediafamily.org

Works to maximize the benefits and minimize the harm of the media on children and families through research, education, and advocacy.

TV-Turnoff Network

1611 Connecticut Avenue, NW, Suite 3A
Washington, DC 20009
1-202-518-5556
www.tvturnoff.org

Encourages children and adults to lessen their TV watching to promote healthier lives and communities.

CHAPTER 11

Safe Surfing
on the Internet

Jessica, a twelve-year-old seventh grader, spends much of her free time on the computer. She designs birthday cards, plays challenging games, gets help online with her homework, communicates with other children around the country, and visits various Internet sites. Most times her surfing is safe and problem-free. Occasionally, however, she encounters material that is disturbing to her. On one occasion she was trying to find a fan site for her favorite member of a new band and typed his name on a search engine. One of the sites she was directed to had nothing to do with the young heartthrob; instead, she was sent to a pornographic site.

While the Internet is a wonderful resource for children, it also poses risks. Children, who are generally trusting of adults and curious about what they see online, are ripe for exploitation through the Internet. Yet many parents develop a false sense of security when their child is online. They may come to believe that she is engaging in an entertaining and harmless exercise. Entertaining? Definitely. Harmless? Not always. Children who surf the Internet are in effect out in public and thus vulnerable to the influences of people they meet online. Not unlike the real world, the virtual world contains inappropriate information, including sexually explicit pictures, violent images, hate-filled messages, and manipulative sales pitches. In the online world it is not uncommon for children to stumble upon this kind of information without seeking it out.

Teens are especially vulnerable to exposure to inappropriate information. They are more likely to use the computer without parental supervision, more likely to participate in discussions on the Internet about personal matters, more likely to seek out inappropriate sites to satisfy their curiosity and sense of adventure, and more likely to make connections with people they meet online but whom they know almost nothing about.

The fact that there are risks to children and teens using the Internet is not an argument for keeping kids off the computer. Rather, what parents need to do is become educated about the risks of the Internet, monitor their children's online experiences, and teach them safeguards for using the Internet. The lessons children learn for surfing the Internet safely—for example, avoiding offensive messages, protecting their privacy, and thinking critically—are lessons that may help them avoid hazards in other aspects of their life. You play an important role in imparting these lessons. This chapter is intended as a guide to help you help your child spend time online in a rewarding, productive, and, most of all, safe manner.

Facts About the Internet

- An estimated 24 million children between the ages of ten and seventeen use the Internet regularly.

- There are approximately 1.5 million sites on the Internet, with thousands more added daily.

- The Center for Media Education indicates that online advertisers target children as young as four.

- The Simon Wiesenthal Center has identified more than fourteen hundred hate sites on the Internet.

- About 6 percent of young people surveyed said they were worried because someone was bothering or harassing them online.

- Approximately one in four children, totaling about 6 million, has received unwanted exposure to sexually explicit pictures while searching for unrelated information.

- As many as one in five children has received unwanted sexual advances from individuals while online.

- According to a recent survey, 20 percent of the youths who received sexual advances online were "very or extremely upset," while 13 percent were "very or extremely afraid."

- On almost a daily basis law enforcement officials arrest what they call a *traveler*—a sexual predator using the Internet to arrange a meeting with an underage child for the purpose of having sex.

Risks to Children on the Internet

While the Internet offers a vast array of information and entertainment for children, it also exposes them to some risks. These stem in part from the Internet's anonymity: you do not always know with whom you are communicating or who is watching in the background. This doesn't mean you should ban your child from using the Internet; after all, the vast majority of its sites are perfectly safe and family friendly. However, it does call for your vigilance and supervision. Here are some of the risks:

UNPRODUCTIVE USE OF TIME. Just as children can spend hours watching television, so, too, can they spend excessive amounts of time on the computer. You may find that your child is spending time online at the expense of homework, family obligations, social activities, outdoor activities, or other interests. Too much time online can restrict her social development and her involvement in other activities.

INVASION OF PRIVACY. Information about your child, such as her name, address, and phone number, can get into the hands of companies as well as people with inappropriate intentions. Many commercial sites for children request personally identifying information from users without first getting approval from parents. While the information may seem to be for harmless purposes such as contests or surveys, companies may use this information to try to sell their products to children.

FINANCIAL HARM. While online a child may be induced to give your credit card information to a company, which can then use that information to your financial detriment. Children may also be misled by online advertising, which can appear as information rather than a commercial.

VERBAL BELLIGERENCE. Children who talk with others in chat rooms may receive insults or obnoxious comments from other computer users.

HARASSMENT OR THREATS. A child may be verbally harassed or threatened while in a chat room, through email, or through bulletin board messages. Surveys indicate that online harassment is not uncommon and can be very upsetting to children.

EXPOSURE TO INAPPROPRIATE INFORMATION. Children may encounter material of a sexual, hateful, or violent nature while on the Internet even though they did not seek this information. They may stumble upon this material by using a search engine that does not filter out inappropriate information or by mistyping the name of a website. And, of course, children may seek these sites intentionally.

EXPOSURE TO INAPPROPRIATE INFLUENCES. Some websites offer information that glamorizes and encourages the use of tobacco, drugs, and alcohol. Others contain information about how to obtain or make weapons or other dangerous devices.

GAMBLING. Internet sites that allow gambling with real money are available. While it is generally illegal for minors to gamble on the Internet, they may nonetheless engage in activities online such as placing wagers or playing lotteries if they have access to a parent's credit card.

PHYSICAL HARM. Children may provide information to other computer users that can lead to face-to-face meetings with them and the risk of physical harm. While rare, there are documented cases of pedophiles who have gained the confidence of children through their computer communications and arranged meetings with them, leading to their physical molestation or abduction. Teens going through emotional difficulties are especially vulnerable to this kind of exploitation.

How to Keep Your Child Safe Online

The surest way to keep your child safe online is to be there with her. But that is not always possible, nor is it always desirable. Just as you may develop rules to protect your child when she deals with strangers, it is important that you establish some guidelines for how she uses the Internet. Bear in mind your child's age when considering the following suggestions:

- Learn how to use the Internet. Adult schools and local colleges may offer courses on computer and Internet use.

- Set some guidelines for your child's Internet use and post them near the computer. These guidelines might include the following:
  - The amount of time she is allowed to use the computer
  - Sites she can go to
  - Topics she is barred from talking about in chat rooms and instant messenger services
  - How to handle requests for personal information
  - What information or incidents she should bring to your attention

- Monitor your child's use of the computer by placing it in a common area of your home such as the family room, living room, or kitchen rather than her bedroom. Pay special attention to the files and games that she downloads. Some computer games can be extremely violent.

- Perhaps the most important principle to convey to your child is not to reveal personal information online.

- You can check to see if your child is giving out personal information online by using a search engine and typing in her name or looking for her name in newsgroups by accessing the site www.deja.com. You may also want to enter your address and phone number on a search engine to see if your child has been giving out this information online.

- Take time to surf the Internet with your child. This is an opportunity not only for you to teach her about responsible use of the Internet but for her to teach you some computer strategies. She can take you to some of her favorite sites while you can show her some sites that relate to her interests or hobbies.

- Consider establishing a rule with your preschool or early elementary school child that she can use the Internet only with an adult.

- Teach your child proper etiquette for using the Internet, which is called *netiquette.* Encourage her to communicate with others in a polite, considerate manner. If necessary, make it clear that threatening anyone online is unacceptable and will result in loss of computer privileges.

- If you find that your child is spending more time online than you think is appropriate, consider setting a timer to limit her computer time.

- Avoid using the computer as a babysitter. Just as excessive television viewing is not healthy for your child, excessive computer use can be harmful as well.

- If your child has set up her own website, make sure the information she posts on it is appropriate. Do not permit her to include personal information that allows her to be contacted.

- Tell your child that she must obtain your approval before she can provide personal information on a website. Check the site's privacy policy before you give permission. You need to find out whether the site rents or sells personal information to advertisers. Also inquire about the privacy policies of your Internet service provider or online service.

- Install software on your computer that blocks access to offensive information on the Internet. (See the section on filtering software on page 236.) Many online services and Internet service providers also offer ways to filter out offensive sites and restrict objectionable email.

- Get to know your child's online friends. This will help you monitor online influences. If she uses America Online, she may have a *buddy list* of individuals that she speaks to on a regular basis and can access easily by computer.

- Tell your child to let you know if she comes across offensive information online. While sexually explicit material is not prohibited on the Internet, child pornography is. You can report sites with child pornography to the National Center for Missing and Exploited Children. (See *Organizations* on page 242.)

- If your child tells you she has received offensive information online, do not blame her, get angry with her, or take away privileges. There is a good chance she received the information through no fault of her own. If you respond in a helpful manner, she will be more likely to come to you if it happens again.

- You can send a copy of an offensive message your child has received to your Internet service provider or online service and ask for its help. The individuals responsible can have their accounts terminated.

- Look for an online service that has a *kids only* area; your child will not encounter offensive or inappropriate material while in this area. America Online has *kids only*, *young teens*, and *mature teens* areas, with different restrictions for each.

- Consider having a joint email address with your child so you can monitor her mail.

- Pay close attention to the chat rooms that your child enters. It is here that children may receive offensive comments or threats. Encourage her to go into chat rooms where she can talk with friends or family members, or rooms that are hosted by responsible adults (www.talkcity.com has moderated sites for children). You may want to sit with her when she is in chat rooms.

- You can use the history function on your browser to see which sites your child has accessed (unless she has figured out how to erase the site references). Both Internet Explorer and Netscape Navigator, two popular browsers, keep a history of sites visited.

- If your child encounters hate sites, use this opportunity to teach her about the dangers and cruelty of hatred and bigotry.

- Let your child know that the people she meets online are strangers and are not always whom they claim to be. Tell her that because she can't see or hear the person she is communicating with, it is very easy for the individual to misrepresent himself. An individual identifying himself as a fifteen-year-old boy may in fact be a forty-year-old man.

- Do not allow your child to arrange a meeting with another computer user without your permission. If you approve the meeting, make sure it takes place in a public area and that you accompany your child.

- Help your child understand consumerism on the Internet. Discuss with her the difference between advertising and educational content. Let her know that just as television commercials may exaggerate the truth, so, too, can companies selling products on the Internet give misleading information. Teach her to be wary of "get rich quick" schemes by quoting the consumer maxim: "If it seems too good to be true, it probably is." When possible, direct your child to websites that do not sell items to children.

- Be clear with your child about the rules for making purchases online. Tell her she is to obtain your permission before purchasing an item. If you have concerns that she may place an order without your approval, do not let her know your credit card number. Monitor your credit card bill for online purchases and check out any unfamiliar numbers on your phone bill.

Rules of the Road on the Information Superhighway

Help your child become netsmart by teaching her to follow these do's and don'ts while online.

- **Do** choose a password that is hard for others to guess but easy for you to remember.
- **Do** treat individuals you meet on the Internet the way you would want to be treated.
- **Do** check the source of information you have received online before acting on it.
- **Do** recognize that when you enter a chat room or an instant message session people will likely see your email address and can thus email you. Consider using a screen name that is different from your email address to remain anonymous. With AOL Instant Messenger you can register a screen name that is different from your AOL screen name.

- **Do** read the policies of your Internet service provider or on-line service to find out how to decrease the number of commercial emails you receive.

- **Do** consider using the feature available with many instant messaging programs, email programs, and chat rooms that allows you to block messages from specific people.

- **Do** consider using a gender-neutral name when talking with others in a chat room. Make sure it does not identify you.

- **Do** tell your parents when you have received a message on the computer that is offensive or upsetting to you. They may decide to contact your Internet service provider or your online service.

- **Do not** give your password to anyone, including a friend, members of a chat group, or someone who claims he is from your Internet service provider or online service. Otherwise, you may find charges on your parents' bill that are not yours.

- **Do not** open email, an email attachment, files, pictures, or games sent by someone you do not know without checking with an adult. Opening an email from an unknown source could harm your computer by exposing it to a virus.

- **Do not** respond to any emails or chat room or bulletin board messages you receive that are offensive or upsetting to you. Either press the "back" key or log off to end the on-line session and then let an adult know.

- **Do not** send information in an email that you want kept confidential. You may find that the recipient has posted your message on a bulletin board.

- **Do not** say anything in a chat room or on a bulletin board that you would not want made public.

- **Do not** send a rude or inconsiderate message to anyone on-line. Internet users have a name for this: flaming.

- **Do not** list your name and email address in a public directory.

- **Do not** enter online contests without first checking with your parents.

- **Do not** disable any filtering software that your parents have installed on the computer. (Some filtering products may indicate in the "log file" that the software has been tampered with.)

- **Do not** arrange a face-to-face meeting with someone you have met online without first getting your parent's approval and having a parent accompany you. Arrange the meeting at a public place such as a restaurant. This will allow you to find out the person's age, gender, and demeanor with minimal risk.

- **Do not** blame yourself or assume you have done something wrong if you receive an offensive message online.

Information Your Child Should Not Reveal Online

Do not give out personal information in a public area on the Internet such as a website, chat room, or bulletin board without your parent's permission. The information you should keep private is as follows:

- Name
- Home address
- Home telephone number
- Social security number
- Email address
- School name and location
- Personal photograph
- Parents' work locations

- Parents' work telephone numbers
- Credit card information

What You Should Know About Parental Control Tools

You can use computer technology to lessen your child's exposure to offensive material on the Internet. The technology works by blocking access to sites that may have inappropriate content. You can do this in three ways: (1) by using a Web browser that has a built-in parental control feature, (2) by signing up with an Internet service provider that filters out this content, or (3) by purchasing a software program that screens out offensive and inappropriate material.

Bear in mind that filtering is an inexact science and as a result no parental control tool is 100 percent reliable. Not only do these tools allow access to some inappropriate material and block access to some appropriate information, but savvy children may be able to bypass the software. The most powerful control tool is parental monitoring and vigilance.

Because filtering programs are not completely effective, you will need to talk with your child about Internet safety issues and continue to supervise her online activities. Before installing the filtering software, find out whether it:

- can be used on your computer.
- works with an Internet service provider.
- functions with a direct Internet connection.
- requires a subscription fee.

If you find that the filtering software you have installed is not working, check to see whether it has been turned off.

Do not install more than one filtering program on your computer at the same time because they can interfere with each other, and do not tell your child that you have installed a filtering system on the computer. You will only invite her to try to get around it.

How Filtering Software Can Protect Your Child

The parental control tools on the market offer a variety of features. Decide which features are important to you and then choose a software program that offers them. These are some of the filtering software features offered:

- Restricts your child's ability to give out personal information.

- Bars access to material on the Internet designated as unsuitable for children.

- Allows access to material designated as appropriate for children.

- Permits you to describe the types of materials your child can access.

- Allows you to establish different Internet limitations for each family member.

- Allows you to monitor your child's online activities by storing the names of sites she has visited and the information she has accessed.

- Shuts down the computer if your child tries to access blocked sites repeatedly.

- Allows you to add or remove sites that can be accessed by your child.

- Limits results of an Internet search to sites appropriate for children.

- Blocks your child's access to chat rooms or allows her to go only to monitored chat rooms.

- Prevents your child from typing in particular words or phrases while she is in a chat room.

- Restricts the amount of time your child is online.

- Prohibits your child from using the computer during a specific time period (such as homework time) or after a specific time.

- Prohibits your child from deleting files from your computer.

- Blocks access by your child to designated software programs on your computer (such as your financial program).

- Prevents your child from receiving email from specific email addresses.

- Prohibits your child from sending email to specific email addresses.

- Blocks the sending or receiving of email with offensive information or personal data.

- Routes email for your child to your email address.

- Prohibits advertising at the top of a Web page.

Filtering Software Programs

The following are popular filtering software programs that you can install on your computer. You can set up the program to block access to sites that contain nudity, sexual content, and hateful and violent material. You may also be able to screen out sites that advocate the use of drugs, alcohol, or tobacco. You can learn more about filtering software by going to www.netparents.org. A comprehensive listing and description of filtering software programs is available at www.safekids.com/filters.htm.

- ADL HateFilter: www.adl.org/hatepatrol/info/default.htm

- Bess: www.bess.net

- Crayon Crawler: www.crayoncrawler.com

- Cyber Patrol: www.cyberpatrol.com/dyn_hm.htm

- CYBERsitter: www.cybersitter.com

- Cyber Snoop: www.pearlsw.com

- KidSafe Explorer: www.arlington.com.au/index.html

- Net Nanny: www.netnanny.com/Default.asp

- SurfWatch: www1.surfwatch.com
- WebSense: www.websense.com/index.cfm

Family-Friendly Internet Service Providers

The following are Internet service providers or online services that have built-in filtering software that blocks access to sites unsuitable for children. Before signing up with one of these providers, check out its filtering criteria to make sure it offers the features you want.

- America Online: www.aol.com
- Dotsafe.com: www.dotsafe.com
- FamilyClick: www.familyclick.com
- Global Family Network: www.familyinternet.myway.com
- GuardiaNet: www.guardianet.net
- Integrity Online: www.integrity.com
- Internet 4 Families: www.i4f.com
- Mayberry USA: www.mbusa.net
- This.com: www.this.com
- ViaFamily: www.ratedg.com/About

Search Engines for Kids

With adult search engines, you run the risk that your child will encounter inappropriate sites. There is virtually no chance of this happening if you have your child use a search engine designed for children, including the following:

- Little Explorers: www.EnchantedLearning.com/Dictionary.html. An easy-to-use search engine for children that offers a picture dictionary with links to related sites.

- One Key: www.onekey.com. Offers an extensive database with more than five hundred categories. It screens out sites that do not meet network television standards.

- SuperSnooper: www.supersnooper.com. Filters out pornographic, violent, and hate-related sites.

- Yahooligans: www.yahooligans.com. A database of about twenty thousand sites that are safe for children. It provides a directory to ease the searching process.

Twenty-five Safe, Entertaining, and Educational Sites for Children

If your child likes to spend time surfing the Web, you can help her use her time constructively by directing her to some child- or teen-oriented websites that offer entertaining and educational content. Sites that you can feel comfortable recommending to your child include the following:

AMERICAN LIBRARY ASSOCIATION: www.ala.org/parents/ index.html. Provides information about children's books (including lists of award-winning books), videotapes, and authors. It also offers games and helps children locate information online.

ARTHUR PAGE: www.pbs.org/wgbh/arthur. A PBS site intended for fans of the popular book and television character created by Marc Brown. It features stories, games, and children's art.

ASK JEEVES FOR KIDS: www.ajkids.com. A search program that enables children to ask questions using everyday language and provides answers on a wide range of topics.

BILL NYE THE SCIENCE GUY: nyelabs.kcts.org. Entertains children online by discussing and demonstrating science concepts in a fun manner and showing highlights of his television show. The site also allows children to email Bill Nye.

BLACK HISTORY SITE: www.kn.pacbell.com/wired/BHM/ AfroAm. Examines African-American issues through a range of activities, including an interactive treasure hunt. It also includes articles about important events in American history relating to African Americans.

CHILDREN'S EXPRESS: www.cenews.org/bureaus.htm. An award-winning site for children in which young people report the news.

CHILDREN'S TELEVISION WORKSHOP: www.ctw.org. Produces *Sesame Street.* Its site features the characters from the long-running program.

THE EXPLORATORIUM: www.exploratorium.edu. Website of the San Francisco science, art, and human perception museum. It offers interactive exhibits on a variety of topics (for example, optical illusions) and allows children to conduct experiments online.

THE FRANKLIN INSTITUTE SCIENCE MUSEUM: sln.fi.edu. Offers entertaining exhibits on a range of science and technology topics. The site includes science, history, and art projects done by children.

FUNBRAIN.COM: www.funbrain.com. Provides enjoyable learning games for children in kindergarten through eighth grade.

GIRL POWER!: www.health.org/gpower/index.htm. A site sponsored by the Department of Health and Human Services intended to empower and encourage girls from ages nine to fourteen to reach their full potential.

KIDS' CASTLE: www.kidscastle.si.edu. The children's site of the Smithsonian Institution. It offers an engaging online tour of the museum's treasures.

LIBRARY OF CONGRESS: www.americaslibrary.gov/cgi-bin/ page.cgi. Offers a fascinating look at America and its past, including famous Americans; favorite pastimes, movies, and songs from long ago; and information about the fifty states. The site also offers a beginner's guide to the Internet.

MISTER ROGERS' NEIGHBORHOOD: www.pbs.org/rogers. An on-line look at the popular television program. It features a tour of the neighborhood, activities for children, lists of children's books on particular themes, songs you can listen to, and a section for parents.

MY VIRTUAL REFERENCE DESK: www.refdesk.com. A bountiful site that provides factual information about virtually any topic imaginable. It offers a search engine and links to a wide variety of reference sources.

NATIONAL AERONAUTICS AND SPACE ADMINISTRATION (NASA): www.nasa.gov. Has a section for children with information and activities about such topics as space and beyond, rockets and airplanes, and astronauts and pioneers. You can view photos from space and even see a launch.

NATIONAL WILDLIFE FEDERATION: www.nwf.org/kids. Sponsor-ed by the environmental magazine *Ranger Rick*. It takes children on tours of different environments such as the wetlands, suggests ideas for outdoor fun, and offers wildlife facts and animal jokes.

NATIONAL ZOO: web2.si.edu/natzoo. Spotlights the Washington, D.C. zoo, featuring an online tour, animal-related games, and movies about animals.

OREGON TRAIL: www.isu.edu/~trinmich/Oregontrail.html. Based on the PBS program, it tells the story of the trail and the brave individuals who traveled it.

PUBLIC BROADCASTING SYSTEM: www.pbs.org. Offers a diverse range of topics, including being president for a day, understanding how the government affects you, tracking the Loch Ness monster, climbing Mount Everest, and exploring the Pyramids.

READING RAINBOW: gpn.unl.edu/rainbow. A site based on the award-winning PBS program for children hosted by LeVar

Burton. It offers areas for children, parents, and teachers. Children can listen to the program's theme song, see a list of upcoming programs, do a variety of activities related to books, and enter writing and art contests.

SCHOOLHOUSE ROCK: genxtvland.simplenet.com/SchoolHouse Rock/index-hi.shtml. Site of the television program. It features academic subjects put to music, including Grammar Rock, Science Rock, Multiplication Rock, and America Rock.

SPORTS ILLUSTRATED FOR KIDS: www.sikids.com. Offers articles, trivia, and videos related to sports.

UNICEF VOICES OF YOUTH: www.unicef.org/voy. Sponsored by the United Nations Children's Fund. It teaches young people about children around the world. Visitors to the site can share ideas regarding world issues and participate in related activities.

ZOOM DINOSAURS: www.EnchantedLearning.com/subjects/dinosaurs/index.html. Tells children everything they want to know and more about these prehistoric reptiles. It can be used by children of different ages and ability levels.

Websites on Safety on the Internet

- www.cyberangels.org
- www.getwise.org
- www.kidsprivacy.org
- www.pedowatch.org
- www.protectkids.com
- www.safekids.com
- www.safeteens.com
- www.smartparent.com

RECOMMENDED READING

Books for Kids

Friday, J., and Mansfield, C. (1998). *101 Cool Sites for Kids on the Net.* Grand Rapids, MI: McGraw-Hill Children's Publishing (for young adults).

Mandel, F. (1999). *Cyberspace for Kids: 600 Sites That Are Kid-Tested and Parent-Approved.* Grand Rapids, MI: McGraw-Hill Children's Publishing.

Pederson, T., and Moss, F. (1999). *Internet for Kids: A Beginner's Guide to Surfing the Net.* Topeka, KS: Econo-Clad Books. (for young adults)

Books for Parents

Aftab, P. (2000). *The Parent's Guide to Protecting Your Children in Cyberspace.* New York: McGraw-Hill.

Brasche, M. (1999). *Child Safety-Net: How to Protect Your Children from Harm Online.* Plantsville, CT: New England Webmasters.

Croft, J. (1999). *Everything You Need to Know About Staying Safe in Cyberspace.* New York: Rosen Publishing Group.

Gralla, P., and Kinkoph, S. (2000). *The Complete Idiot's Guide to Protecting Your Child Online.* Indianapolis, IN: Que.

Hughes, D. R. (1998). *Kids Online: Protecting Your Children in Cyberspace.* Grand Rapids, MI: Fleming H. Revell Co.

Maynard, R. (2000). *Goodparents.Com: What Every Good Parent Should Know About the Internet.* Amherst, NY: Prometheus Books.

ORGANIZATIONS

Enough is Enough

P. O. Box 26228
Santa Ana, CA 92799
1-888-2Enough (1-888-236-6844)
www.enough.org

Strives to make the Internet safer for children and families by informing the public of the dangers of online pornography and sexual predators.

The National Center for Missing and Exploited Children

Charles B. Wang International Children's Building
699 Prince Street
Alexandria, VA 22314
1-703-274-3900
1-800-THE-LOST (1-800-843-5678)
www.missingkids.com

> *The toll-free hotline is available twenty-four hours a day for those who have information on missing or exploited children. Internet sites containing child pornography should also be reported to this organization.*

The Simon Wiesenthal Center

1399 South Roxbury Drive
Los Angeles, CA 90035
1-800-900-9036
www.wiesenthal.com

> *Combats bigotry throughout the world, including the use of the Internet by hate groups to disseminate their message.*

Index